I0460042

SELF COACH TENNIS

SELF COACH TENNIS

How To Be Your Own Best Self Coach

Neal Newman, Ph.D.

Copyright © 2025 by Neal Newman

All rights reserved. No part of this book may be reproduced or transmitted in any form or by any means, electronic or mechanical, including photocopying, recording, or by any information storage and retrieval system, except in the case of brief quotations embodied in critical articles and reviews, without prior written permission of the publisher.

Printed in the United States of America

ISBN Paperback: 979-8-9926973-0-8
ISBN Ebook: 979-8-9926973-1-5

Interior Design: Creative Publishing Book Design

I hope this training will help a lot of people,
but I would like to dedicate it to my daughter Jen,
son Cole and his wife Becky, and my grandson, Caiden.

I hope the lessons learned in this training will help them have the
self coaching tools that enable them to have fulfilling experiences and
performances in tennis, if they so choose, and in life in general.

Table of Contents

Acknowledgments xi

Preface xiii

**Chapter 1—Introduction to this Training on Self Coaching
and the Mental Game**. 1
Importance of the Mental Game. 3
What are the Goals of the Mental Game. 4

**Chapter 2—Self Coaching Training: Self Management
through the Self, Self-Coach, and the Self-Self-Coach
Relationship**. 9
Self 9
Self-Coach 10
The 3 Dimensional Model of the Self-Coach 10
Self Support 10
Self Activation 11
Self Direction 12
Self-Self Coach Relationship 15

Chapter 3—Self Coaching Experience Organizing Model. 19
NLP Outcome Frame 19
Additional Self Coaching Experience Organizing Models . . . 26
Variation on NLP Outcome Frame 26

The Gestalt Cycle of Experience organizing model 27

Gestalt Therapy Concepts organizing model. 29

Milton Erickson Therapy Concept : Utilization 31

Self Coaching with the Unconscious. 33

Rossi's Four Stage Creative Process 35

Rossi's Ideomotor Approach 36

Summary and Importance of Using an Experience
Organizing Model. 38

Chapter 4—Self Coaching Perspectives 41

List Of Self Coaching Perspectives 41

How to Select a Self Coaching Perspective 56

Being in a Frame of Mind. 57

Chapter 5—Mental Skills Training. 59

The D-E-E-P Approach to Self Coaching and Mental
Skills Training. 60

Self Coaching Tools: Mental Skills Training 61

Chapter 6—Mental State Training 77

Core Individual Mental States. 79

Combining the Mental States 89

Sequencing the Mental States 90

The Difference Procedure. 91

The 5 Ingredients Optimal Mental State. 97

Quick Fixes for Mental State Adjustments 99

Self Coaching and PAR, Flow and the Transcendent Peak
Experience/Performance 101

My Mental State (MS) Notes 103

Mental State Playing Inventory. 104

Playing Level Scale 106

Chapter 7—Self Coaching: The Tennis Performance Categories..109

Identifying the Tennis Performance Categories 110

Tennis Performance Categories Checklist 114

Chapter: 8—The PAR Approach: Self Coaching and the PAR Approach to the Event Management Sequence...119

Prepare 120

Adjust...134

Review 144

The Par Approach to the Event Management Sequence

Summary 147

Self Coach Tennis (SCT) Rating Scale 150

Chapter 9—Self Coaching With Mental Game Issues.......155

Chapter 10—Conclusion and Moving Forward: Be Your Own Best Self Coach and Play Self Coach Tennis.............................169

Checklists and Rating Scales............................173

Tennis Performance Categories Checklist 174

Mental State Playing Inventory.......................183

Playing Level Scale 185

Self Coaching Tennis (SCT) Rating Scale 188

Acknowledgments

I would first and foremost like to thank my beloved wife, Rayna, for her consistent support for my tennis and psychology careers over the years. She has allowed me the time to pursue and develop my interests and talents. Best wife ever! I would be lost without her (and not just because I have a bad sense of direction). I also owe everything to my mom, Mildred, for raising me in such a fun, ego supportive way! And thank you to her and my wise, thoughtful, step-dad, Bernie, both of whom are my role models for how to be as a person. They are Mildred Newman and Bernard Berkowitz, psychoanalysts and co-authors of *How to be your own best friend*, a NY Times bestseller. In some ways I humbly and hopefully see this book on *Self Coach Tennis: How to be your own best self coach*, as following in their footsteps of helping people be good to themselves and support and guide themselves effectively.

I would also like to thank all my doubles partners and tennis friends, who have been such a vital part of my tennis journey. I won most of my USTA national doubles titles with Phil Landauer, Larry Turville and my son, Cole, so I especially acknowledge them here. I really appreciate all the time and playing we did together. I also would like to acknowledge my long time good friend and psychology colleague, Jerry Stern, who did sport psychology with me in our early days, and did NLP and Ericksonian training with me.

Preface

I view the training in this book as being in the tradition of a book written by my Mom and Stepdad, Mildred Newman and Bernard Berkowitz. They co-wrote *How To Be Your Own Best Friend.* In their book they helped people have permission to be good to themselves. Before that book, published in 1971, many people believed it was selfish to be self compassionate. Since that was published, people now more commonly believe that it is a good idea to treat oneself well, and that in fact, if one feels ok it may make it easier to be helpful and thoughtful to others, as well as oneself. In my therapy and performance enhancement practice as a psychologist, I rarely find I have to convince others that it is permissible and healthy to treat themselves well. Sometimes, people know it's a good idea to treat themselves well but they don't feel like they deserve it. More often it seems like people are missing the knowledge and skills about how to manage their experience well. They don't know how to treat themselves compassionately or coach themselves effectively.

I have written this book to share my mental game training program with you. This will provide you with the tools (models, perspectives, mental skills, mental states) you need to be your own best Self Coach. This training has helped lots of tennis players, as well as other athletes, musicians, and the general population. Here, though, I will primarily speak to tennis players. The idea is that being your own best Self Coach will boost your experience and performance in tennis and life.

My Self Coaching ideas have sure helped me. I went from a person who played no Junior events, and played small college tennis at Earlham College, to a player who won 40 USTA senior national doubles and 4 ITF senior world doubles events, in addition to representing the USA in international events that won 2 ITF world team championships. This included having to deal with numerous health and physical issues. Believe me, my mental game training helped a lot in developing and performing up to potential. I used to tell my close friend and doubles partner, Phil Landauer, that with his strokes and my sense of humor we could play well together. He said I had improved more than anyone else he had seen.

Developing and monitoring your Self Coach abilities means you will be playing Self Coach Tennis. This is where you can focus on giving yourself a Self Coach grade while playing in addition to a playing grade.

Enjoy the journey of learning to be your own Self Coach. I hope you will commit to playing Self Coach tennis.

CHAPTER 1

Introduction to this Training On Self Coaching and the Mental Game

I would like to work with you on learning a new approach to tennis—and life! This involves learning to be both a Self as Player AND Self as Self Coach who work together to help you manage your playing and life experiences. Imagine having your best coach with you to help you make good choices and be in a positive frame of mind and mental state as you play tennis, and play life. You can learn to be that coach to yourself! There is learning to be done, practicing to be done, to cultivate the skills and perspectives that will help you learn how to be the best you you can be. It is worth it. This can change and improve your life!

Welcome to my mental training program for learning to be your own best Self Coach. There are skills and perspectives we can learn that will help us perform up to our ability, have a positive experience and be the person we want to be. In this training, I will focus mainly on learning to work with yourself as a tennis player, but we can also apply these learnings to other performances and life. When we run into difficulty with how we are playing, we often disconnect from our inner resources. The skills and perspectives we work on here will help you discover how to connect and reconnect to the person and player you want to be.

How do I happen to be writing this book? My Mom and Step-Dad, Mildred Newman and Bernard Berkowitz, were psychologists and psychoanalysts in New York City who co-wrote the best seller, How To Be Your Own Best Friend. They were trailblazers in helping people understand how it is ok to talk with yourself positively and be good to yourself. Now this is well accepted. The book was great at each person getting out of it what they needed. My training here is perhaps a more systematic training in offering very useful tools for facilitating your own performance and experience.

I am a psychologist, with a Ph.D. in Counseling Psychology from Ohio State University, along with extensive experience in NLP (Neuro-Linguistic Programming), Gestalt Therapy, Ericksonian Approaches, and sport/performance psychology. As a tennis player I have won 40 USTA national doubles titles, 4 ITF world doubles titles, and represented the US in international competition numerous times, including being on 2 teams that won the ITF world team championship for my age group. I have been ranked #1 in the country in my age group nationally in doubles across multiple age groups and in father-son tennis, with my son, Cole. I was inducted into the USTA Midwest Hall of Fame in 2015. I have worked with athletes for many years, in private practice and as part of my work first at the Ohio State University Mental Health Clinic and later at the OSU Counseling and Consultation Service. I also taught a music performance enhancement seminar at Ohio State University for years. I have some music background, having attended the High School of Music & Art (now LaGuardia High School) in New York City. I tell you the above to help provide some credibility for my offering this training. Over the years, I have drawn on my psychology background and playing background to come up with some very practical and useful ideas for helping you be at your best.

The mental training program I am offering you here will include sections on Self Coaching. We will discuss the qualities of the Self

Coach, and the Self-Self Coach relationship process. I will train you on having an Experience Organizing Model for you to use in processing your experience. We will review a core list of Self Coaching Perspectives that help put you in a useful frame of mind. Learning how to monitor and coach yourself on the Performance Categories will also be an important part of your Self Coaching training. We will also do practical Mental Skills training for you to be able to use your sensory resources, and cultivate Relaxation Skills and protective devices that will help you handle experiences. I will teach you my D-E-E-P approach to learning Relaxation Skills. We will then do more extensive Mental State training, for you to learn about a variety of core mental states and how to access an optimal performance state while playing. Once you have learned the core mental training skills and perspectives, we can put them together in the P-A-R (Prepare-Adjust-Review) approach to the Event Management Sequence. You can have strategies/routines that you can rely on to play at your best. We can also review ways to overcome some common psychological obstacles that can occur while playing.

Learning to be your own best Self Coach is learning to develop your Mental Game. I am hoping you will embrace learning the Mental Game, just as you are motivated to develop your tennis skills as a player. It is helpful to commit to being a student of the Mental Game. When your mental game is good, you are more apt to play up to your abilities and have a positive experience. I suggest you set process goals for your Mental Game in practice and matches. You can give yourself a Self Coaching/Mental Game grade after a match, just like you have a tennis game match score.

IMPORTANCE OF THE MENTAL GAME

What does it take to play a good tennis match? Why is the mental game important?

3

To play tennis well we certainly need to learn to hit the ball and develop the variety of strokes that tennis players have: forehand, backhand, serve, returns, volleys, overhead, drop shot, different spins and different heights of hitting the ball, etc.. We also need to learn how to set up a point and anticipate opponent shots. So there is strategy and anticipation. There are decisions to make about the strokes we select and our strategies for playing an opponent. This is all part of self management. We also all have our own emotions and psychology to deal with. How do we manage our mental state? How does our drive to win and fear of losing affect us, if at all? Do our own issues within ourselves and relating with others affect our performance? How do we handle pressure points in a match? How do we deal with players who we think are better than us, or equal yet hard to beat? How do we manage physical injury or physical limitations at a certain time, including fatigue? You can see there is a lot of self management needed to do a good job managing a match. That self management is what we are calling the mental game here.

WHAT ARE THE GOALS OF THE MENTAL GAME

I think we want a positive mental game to help us:

1) **Play well**—We want to be able to at least play up to our ability. Not underperform. We want to help ourselves play even better than our typical good game if we can. Before a recent US Open match, Medvedev said he would need to play 12 out of 10 to beat Alcaraz, and he did. That means he was able to get in a really good space and access his best game. Do you tend to under-perform, or not consistently play at the level to which you are capable? Developing your Self Coaching and Mental Game can help you play at your best.

2) **Have a positive experience**—We want to enjoy playing and have a positive experience. We don't play tennis to be miserable

4

and give ourselves a hard time. We play for the love of the game. Let's remember to enjoy our process of playing. That is a healthy way to approach playing, and is also apt to help us access a mental state that enables us to play well. Learning how to hold on to the perspective of the joy of playing, can help us deal with adversity and frustrations that can occur in a match. Learning to embrace the challenges of playing can help you enjoy the process. Do you tend to have a positive experience when you play, or is this something you can focus on?

3) **Improve**—Let's be smart about our development as a player. We can be a student of the game. As a player with a strong mental game, what do I need to do to get better, and improve my tennis results. When I was in my late 30's I developed a two handed backhand that helped me go on to win numerous national and world doubles titles. I had gone to nationals and seen what the top players did. I could see it would help to have a two handed backhand to especially go against some top servers and players attacking the backhand. My results dramatically improved with the addition of the two handed backhanded. If you look at professional sports, you will see how the top players had great talent, but also developed parts of their game to improve. Lebron James, in basketball, improved his inside post up game and outside shooting. In tennis, Ivan Lendl got fitter and that made a huge difference to him getting over the hump to win major titles. It seemed like Rafael Nadal kept improving after already being a top player—improving his serve, volleys, etc.. Novak Djokovic went gluten free with his diet to feel better and play better. What do you need to improve? How many players of all ages play for years without improving their game? Even at older ages, you can still cultivate improved strokes, be better at devising and implementing a game plan, and learn to

5

manage your mental state better while playing. What can you do to improve?

4) **Be the person I want to be**—I have wanted to play well and accomplish things on the tennis court. But that has never been more important than being the person I want to be on the court. I want to compete well and do my best, but all while being a good person and treating others well. I heard Roger Federer once spoke with an elementary school class, and told them it's nice to be important, but it's more important to be nice. My mom, Mildred Newman, a well known psychoanalyst, and co- author of How To Be Your Own Best Friend, was very empathic of people having worries and problems, but added it was most important to show good character. My favorite story is about my son, Cole. He was a state high school doubles champion in Ohio, and a college All American at Denison University. When he was playing in junior tournaments, where rankings tended to be of some import to players, he was in a tournament at a local club. One of my co-workers at Ohio State University told me his son said Cole was his hero. I said what did he do? He said Cole had been in a close match on a hot day, and his opponent had started to cramp. The tournament director came over to see the condition of the player, giving him a certain amount of time to recover. After a little while, the player couldn't quite continue and the tournament referee was about to disqualify him. Cole suddenly came up to the ref, and asked if he could take his bathroom break now. He then got some Gatorade for his opponent. With a few minutes extra time and the Gatorade, the player could continue, and actually won the second set. Cole won the match in 3 sets. He didn't even tell me about what he did when he came home that day, but confirmed it when my colleague at work told me about it. The field of positive

psychology, developed by Martin Seligman and his colleagues, speaks about the character strengths and virtues that contribute to a sense of flourishing and a meaningful life. Being wise, creative, curious, brave, persevering, honest, fair, humble, empathic, loving, and humorous are just some of the qualities described. See the book, *Character Strengths and Virtues,* by Seligman and Petersen, for a more in depth discussion. Playing tennis is a forum and opportunity for you to build and demonstrate your own character. Are you being the person you want to be on the tennis court, and in life? What can you do to compete, play and relate in a way that you can feel good about yourself?

Learning to be your own best Self Coach can help you have a strong mental game, and accomplish the goals just stated. So let's get started with the Self Coaching training.

CHAPTER 2

Self Coaching Training

Self Management through the *Self, Self-Coach,* and the *Self—Self Coach Relationship*

I assume you want to play well, and that having a good mental game will increase the chances of that happening. How do we do the self managing that helps you play well? The model I am proposing has you having/being a SELF, and having/being a SELF COACH. You are both. And the both of you can interact to help you have access to your playing resources. When we don't play well, we seem to lose some kind of connection to ourselves and our resources. So you know how to hit a forehand, but somehow, in the middle of a match, you suddenly can't seem to hit it right. You have lost some connection to the knowing of how to hit it. Your Confidence lowers, and you seem to lose technique with your stroke. How do we gain and regain access to how to play? It helps for the Self and Self Coach to communicate to find the resource and be able to hit the forehand again. In this chapter we will address the qualities of the Self and Self Coach, and how they communicate with each other. In future chapters we will address learning a variety of perspectives and skills that comprise the wisdom of the Self and Self Coach.

SELF

Your Self is your sense of "I". When I am speaking to myself, and I say "I would like to…", that is my Self speaking. The Self is your seat

9

of awareness of what is going with you. "I am aware of…". Within your Self you also have your lifetime of resources and experiences. As such, your Self contains your unconscious as well as conscious resources. As I go inside and examine my reactions, feelings, hopes, thoughts, etc., that is my Self talking. As I play, I hit my tennis shot. Sometimes, however, your Self can lose connection with itself. When upset, or in the stress of the moment, there may be internal noise that interferes with the Self being able to guide itself. To regain positive self connection and guide oneself more effectively, it may be helpful to be able to get some distance and perspective from the difficulties of the moment. That is where the Self-Coach can be helpful.

SELF COACH

Your Self Coach is your wise, validating, empathic, facilitative, resourceful part of yourself. Its mission is to work with the Self to help you have a good life and accomplish the goals of the mental game in tennis and life: positive experiences, good performances, improving and being a good person. Being a positive sponsor and facilitator, it helps the Self locate and connect to needed resources.. The Self Coach does this via providing 3 primary functions that I call the 3 Dimensional Model of the Self Coach, described below:

FUNCTIONS OF THE SELF COACH:
THE 3 DIMENSIONAL MODEL OF THE SELF COACH

The 3 Dimensional Model includes the Self Coach having Self Support, Self Activation, and Self Direction functions.

SELF SUPPORT—Self Support refers to the compassion and foundation of strength you can provide yourself by being physically, emotionally, and mentally prepared to do an activity. Often it is helpful to have a certain amount of relaxation, patience and confidence in order to feel able to approach a situation effectively. Self Support is based on awareness and compassion. Laura Perls, one of the key figures in gestalt therapy, and the wife of Fritz Perls, emphasized how you need sufficient self support in order to handle life challenges. As examples, you can support yourself with ego supportive words or images, and can support yourself with breathing, muscle relaxation and a grounded physical stance. If you wanted to lift something heavy, you would need to support the lifting by getting into a grounded posture. Self Acceptance is a cornerstone of Self Support. Allowing yourself to be who you are, allowing yourself to make mistakes and being open to learning and developing, is an essential component of coaching yourself effectively. In a recent interview about his mental game, Novak Djokovic spoke about being self accepting about whatever was happening in a match, and then placing his attention on being present in the moment. I like the idea of using the "that's ok" response. While playing a tournament match, when I miss a shot, say a backhand return, I like to say "that's ok" to myself, after which I picture correcting the shot so that I can hit it better next time. Then I turn to ready myself for the next point.

SELF ACTIVATION—Self Activation refers to the energy and conglomeration of mental states (eg. Motivation, Determination, Concentration, Enjoyment) that help you mobilize yourself to accomplish your goals. Jim Loehr speaks to the importance of being fully activated in his book, *The Power of Full Engagement*. Gestalt therapy speaks of mobilizing one's energy as an important part of the gestalt cycle of experience involving healthy contact. The Gestalt Institute of Cleveland promotes this gestalt cycle of experience, showing how a person with healthy experiencing, experiences Sensation (eg. pangs in the stomach), then Awareness (eg aware the pangs suggest hunger), then Mobilizes Energy (eg. internal building toward movement), then engages in Action (eg. walks to the refrigerator and selects an apple), then makes Contact (eg. chews the apple), then Withdraws (eg. satiated after eating the apple), and now ready for the next experience. Csiksentmihalyi, in *Flow*, writes about the value of doing activities for their own sake, and being enjoying and focused, as part of the ingredients of the flow experience. The person is activated here by the sense of enjoyment and concentrated immersion in the experience.

SELF DIRECTION—This function of Self Coaching involves helping one's self move towards one goals. This involves being able to take the action steps that will help one reach one's goals. This includes the ability to set an outcome and implement a plan. NLP (Neuro-Linguistic Programming) speaks of the importance of outcomes being set up that are sensory based, testable, stated in positives, and initiated by the person. The NLP Outcome Frame teaches us that it is useful to have an outcome in mind. When I was doing my training in Gestalt Therapy at the Gestalt Institute of Cleveland, Sonia Nevis would say that therapy is a search for a Theme. When we identify a theme, we have something figural which emerges, which helps us select ways to experiment with our experience. Once we identify a theme, we create some direction, some focus for our work. In terms of Mental States, Motivation, having to do with a person's goals, can be experienced as a source of Self Activation and a source of Self Direction. The state immersion/saturation component of Concentration can be activating, but there is also a directional component to Concentration, which involves the idea of being focused on some item of interest. As such, we see that various Mental States can involve different components of the 3 Dimensional Model.

Here is a diagram that depicts this 3 Dimensional Model of Self Coaching:

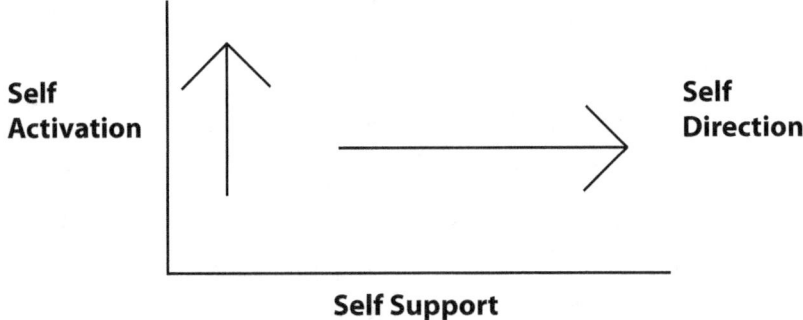

Self Activation

Self Direction

Self Support

So we see that the Self Coach supports the Self and works with the Self to activate and direct the Self. The Self Coach can here be viewed as a wise, inner part of the Self that has access to inner wisdom, and serves as a facilitator that helps the Self be the way he/she wants to be.

Location of the Self Coach: Now we know the functions of the Self Coach. The question now becomes where is the Self Coach located in relation to the Self? It is helpful to experience the Self Coach as an embodied presence, not just an abstract idea. You can experience the Self Coach in the same approximate space as the Self or project it outside of of yourself or somewhere else inside of yourself. Each person can select the location of the Self Coach that works for them. The important part is to have the Self Coach present and available. Too often, many players have the Self playing with the Self Coach absent, and then they don't make the best choices or adjustments during the event process. Playing Self Coach Tennis means we set a process goal of having our Self Coach available to work with the Self.

Some people like to locate their Self-Coach part within themselves where they have the Self and Self Coach in about the same place:

Self: I am having trouble with my serve

Self-Coach: I think it may be a good idea to look at the mechanics. It could be helpful to slow down the motion, toss a little higher, keep my head still, or add a little more spin?

Self: As I look at it, I think I'll take my time and add a little more spin.

Here the Self and Self Coach are located inside the self in a similar location but both parts are working together to stay connected to resources. There is "I" language here. Some people find this the most natural way to Self Coach. They access their Self Coach in the same space as the Self. They can be in the tennis game as a Player and in the game as a Self Coach from within the same space. They can access their resources this way. They are not separating their Self and Self Coach into as distinct separate location parts, but the person understands "I am both the experiencing Self AND the managing experience Self". With Self and Self Coach together, it is also possible to step back for perspective at times. This can work well for them. They may not be comfortable with or accustomed to the therapeutic dissociation that can occur when you separate the parts more distinctly. A possible problem with not separating the parts so much, though, is that if the Self is upset about something, the internal noise that creates can result in them disconnecting from their resources. Have you ever been in group therapy? An individual in the group is often very smart about helping others with their problems, but when the person has a similar issue they are not as resourceful. Getting some distance from the problem seems to help with perspective and problem solving. As such, I think it can work well to locate the Self Coach in a space outside the Self, where the Self Coach can see the Self as an Other. The Self Coach can then readily support and guide you like speaking to a friend in need. Doing it this way, you can think of your Self Coach as being in a specific physical location, rather than just thinking of it abstractly. Right now, how about conjuring up your own wise, validating, facilitative, resourceful Self Coach. Do you locate it to your right, to your left, in front, behind, or inside of you somewhere? Wherever you locate your Self Coach in space, it helps your dialogue with your Self if you have the felt presence of the Self Coach. The Self Coach sees and senses the Self as an other, so will say things like:

> Self Coach: I notice you are struggling with your forehand now. What is going on?

> Self: Yes. I missed the last few forehands, and now I am backing off hitting it.

> Self Coach: You have lost Confidence in it right now? Is it a Confidence issue or technical stroke issue?

> Self: It may be both. I think I need to reconnect to my forehand.

> Self Coach: Would it help you to image hitting it the way you like, seeing if that can help you find your timing and Confidence?

> Self: I'll try it.............(picturing the forehand 8 times)..... Yes. That is helping. I feel more tuned in to my stroke now.

Notice the Self Coach talks to the Self as "you" or "we" here, with the Self being as an other.

SELF—SELF COACH RELATIONSHIP

We have examined the nature of the Self and the Self Coach. The above examples also show us some things about how the Self as Player and Self as Self Coach communicate when the Self Coach is in different locations. Now let's explore the nature of the Self—Self Coach Relationship some more. The Self and Self Coach can together consider how to prepare for the match, how to play the match with the optimal mental state, strokes and game plan, how to make adjustments as needed during the match, and how to review the match afterwards and set goals for the next match. While the Self Coach is wise and has access to your playing resources, the relationship between Self and Self Coach tends to work well when the Self Coach is validating and facilitative. The

Self doesn't always want to be told what to do, but there are times the Self appreciates it.

By validating, I mean the Self Coach is a witness of the Self, who can empathically see, hear and sense what is going on with the self. For example, if you are upset about missing a couple of backhand returns, the Self Coach could notice that, and say, "I notice you just got upset after missing your backhand return. What is going on?" Once validating, the Self Coach can facilitate the Self responding to the situation as effectively as possible. "Shall we take a look at what's going on with the return? Can we first say, "that's ok", to be Self Accepting that we miss a shot?

Then can we assess whether the problem is with our mental state readiness, stroke technique, or court positioning, or something else? What do you notice?" The Self might say, " I feel like the serve is hitting me in a bad spot, jamming me." Or "I'm not getting in my return stance like I prefer". Or "I'm feeling too frustrated, and need to clear my head to be fully ready for the next shot". The Self Coach can then ask the Self what you need to do, or what we need to do, to adjust as this time.

The task is to find the needed resource and make the adjustment. The temptation for some people is to have the Self Coach be like a parental figure. The nurturing, encouraging and praising component of that can at times be helpful, but there is the danger of the Self not liking it if the Self Coach is too imposing. The relationship between the Self and Self Coach can best be viewed as collaborative and dialogical, so that either the Self or Self Coach can come up with a creative idea about how to handle a situation. The Self Coach as facilitator can help the Self maintain a healthy perspective and process the experience using relevant mental skills. Having a wise perspective, the Self Coach can help keep the Self focused on goals or relevant issues, while being compassionate and helping the Self maintain a sense of humor or playfulness as fitting the circumstance.

To illustrate the Self—Self Coach Relationship, let me show you an internal dialogue I could go through, to ensure you are understanding what you have been reading in this chapter so far:

Self: I'm feeling eager to get my ideas across to the reader, but am not sure if I am giving the reader enough examples to comprehend my points.

Self Coach: Neal, your energy seems fine, but you are not sure if what you're writing is expressing your ideas in a practical enough way?

Self: Yes, I am enjoying writing my ideas down, but I am not sure if a person new to this will get the idea.

Self Coach: Any sense of what you need right now?

Self: Maybe I can review what I have been writing, reading it from the perspective of someone new to the material. Then I can hopefully tell if I am communicating this information in a useful way. Maybe I could write an example?

Self Coach: So, you feel ok about that plan?

Self: Yes. That seems like a good way to start.

Now, to give a tennis example of the Self—Self Coach dialogue. In this example, a player is struggling to hold serve, and is frustrated.

Self Coach: I notice you are having trouble holding serve. What is going on?

Self: I am missing too many first serves, and my opponent is putting away my second serve.

Self Coach: Can you take a little something off of your first serve, or do you need to change how you are hitting it in terms of technique?

Self: I think I can hit the first serve with a little more spin. Hitting it less flat should increase my first serve percentage.

Self Coach: What can you do so you do better on second serve points, when needed.

Self: I can be more mindful about serving the second serve into the backhand.

Self Coach: Ok. Ready to go now?

Self: Yes. It feels good to have a plan.

Now that you have a sense of how the Self and Self Coach communicate, let's turn to an Experience Organizing Model that can help you process whatever you are experiencing in an event.

CHAPTER 3

Self Coaching
Experience Organizing Model

So far we have decided we want to have a good mental game, and to get that we want to cultivate our Self Coaching ability. To start that we have discussed being both a Self and a Self Coach and the way the Self and Self Coach can relate to connect to resources and reach goals. To coach yourself well it is important to have a model that helps you make sense of your experience. I am calling this the idea of having a Self Coaching Experience Organizing Model. If we don't have this it will be more difficult to manage our experience.

In this chapter I am going to start by presenting you with an easy to use Experience Organizing Model. The model I encourage you to use is taken from Neuro-Linguistic Programming (NLP). It is called the NLP Outcome Frame. I am going to teach you this here so you can use this model to process your ongoing experience. I will then present you with some additional ways to work with your experience. It helps to have a variety of ways to work with your experience and access your resources.

NLP OUTCOME FRAME

The basic elements of the NLP Outcome Frame are that in the moment you are in a Present State, can decide on your Desired State, and then need to find and use Resources that will help you move from your Present State to your Desired State.

PRESENT STATE—To identify your Present State, you need Awareness of how things are in the moment. This can be awareness of your feelings, thoughts and behavior, and any issues going on. To apply to tennis, you can be aware of how things are going with your Mental State, Strokes, Game Plan, Physical State, Relationship with your opponent or doubles partner or others, or any other things that apply to where you are in the moment. **Awareness** is key here. Your Self and Self Coach can work together to increase awareness of what is going on. Sometimes when playing, the Self can get caught up in the moment and not realize what is going on. The Self Coach, being a wise observer, may notice you seem to be missing a lot of serves, or seem frustrated with how you are playing. The Self and Self Coach can then dialogue about what is going on. It helps to approach awareness of your Present State with a curious, nonjudgmental attitude. It is important to appreciate what you detect, rather than be lamenting and self critical.

DESIRED STATE—Once you know your Present State it is important to decide what your Desired State is. This is where and how you would like to be. This is identifying what you want. Your Desired State involves **Goal Setting.** To do good goal setting it is recommended that you state things that are sensory based, doable, stated in the positive, and initiated by self. So, rather than say "don't be tense", it is preferred to say "relax my arm". There are certain basic information gathering questions you can ask yourself:

1. What do I want?
2. When/where where do I want it?
3. What will it look like, sound like, or feel like to get the outcome?

The key I'd like you to understand here is that your focus is on how you want to be and play, and not on being upset about where you are in your Present State. The Self and Self Coach can work together to determine what your Desired State is. If you are missing a lot of first serves, the Self and Self Coach can determine the goal is getting a higher percentage of first serves in.

RESOURCES—Once you know what you want and how you'd like to be, your task is to figure out how to get there. How can I go from where I am to how I would like to be? These are the Resources. This can mean connecting to inner resources already developed or developing internal resources, or finding external resources that will help me reach my desired outcome. If I miss a shot because I am worried about losing the point or the match, I may already know how to take the pressure off of myself with a wise Perspective or know how to relax my arm, or I may need to better learn how to do it. If my arm is tight because of slight muscle soreness, maybe going to an external resource like putting on a brace, or using a massage gun would help. If I am injured consulting with a doctor or physical therapist is another example of contacting an external resource.

Rather than be self critical, my task is to be flexible in my thinking and allow myself to **Experiment** with ways to move from my Present State to Desired State. It may take adding different or additional ideas before you get to the Desired State. That is fine. As the old story goes, Thomas Edison was asked how he invented the light bulb when there were so many failed experiments. He replied, there were no failed experiments. It takes 500 experiments to invent the light bulb. You are unlikely to need 500 experiments to make an effective adjustment while playing, but be open to the possibility you may need to try more than one thing. You experiment with adding a Resource, and the effect of that is feedback telling you whether you are now in your Desired State or whether you need to try something else. For example, the Self and Self Coach can discuss whether to add more spin to the first serve. If that doesn't get you your outcome you can try lowering your toss because it is a windy day, or take your time and focus on your contact point.

Please do realize that if you are already doing well, and your Present State = Desired State, you don't need to search for more Resources. Just keep playing as you are.

There is another way to think about going from where I am to where I want to be. Sometimes, rather than move from one Mental State to another improved one, I may want to move from a current Problem to a Goal. My Problem could be I am not using my legs enough on my strokes and my Goal could be to use my legs. The Resource could be to focus on using my legs with each stroke. This is a Performance Skill issue where we are focusing on the technical skill of using our legs well with our strokes. I can think of this as a Problem and Goal. Alternatively, this could be a Concentration issue, where the issue isn't about my knowing stroke technique as much as it is in being fully present and focused. In this case the Present State would be low Concentration and the Desired State would be to have positive Concentration. So, in one case we can think of Problem and Goal, while in another we might view it in terms of Present State and Desired State. To illustrate the possibility of viewing it either way, see the diagram below:

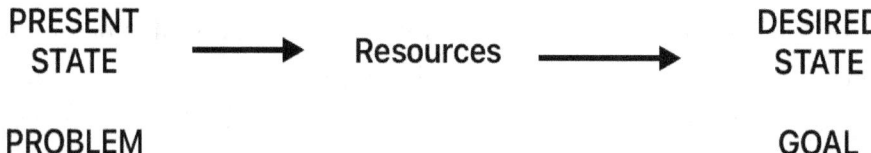

PRESENT STATE → Resources → **DESIRED STATE**

PROBLEM   **GOAL**

Practical Examples of Using the NLP Outcome Frame—Here are a few examples of using the NLP Outcome Frame, to help you understand how to use it.

1. *Issue:* A player is self critical about missing a shot:
   Present State/Problem: Missing shot; Self critical

Desired State/Goal: Fix stroke; Be supportive of self; Orient toward Desired State or Goal

Resource: Select positive Perspective: be in Learning Frame - allowed to miss shots; Mentally rehearse fixing stroke rather than lamenting the miss; image hitting it the way you want;

2. *Issue:* A player is not warmed up enough at the beginning of the match

   Present State/Problem: not physically ready to play; didn't do any warmup

   Desired State/Goal: be physically ready

   Resources: do warmup routine

3. *Issue:* A player is not adjusting to a game plan that is not working well; not moving a slow opponent around; hitting steady but not with variety like adding in lobs, drop shots, and hitting away from the opponent

   Present State/Problem: Not adjusting; Game plan not working; not moving a slow opponent around;

   Desired State/Problem: Make needed adjustments - hit lobs, drop shots and look to make opponent move

   Resources: Change game plan; Picture hitting a different variety of shots; Make sure you access your Self Coach, to help you make adjustments during the match.

4. *Issue:* A player is playing poorly. His or her timing is off; not in a good mental state

   Present State: underperforming; timing is off; negative mental state

   Desired State: regain timing; access positive mental state

   Resources: Adopt a Self Accepting perspective; Focus on your Process; Picture your strokes with repetition to regain timing; Identify and access your optimal mental state. (There is training on this in the Mental State Training chapter.)

Personal Examples

In each match we are faced with challenges that we need to coach ourselves through. In my 30's I played Curt Josselyn, the Ohio high school state champion, who went on to become the top player in the Mid American Conference. He was very talented and hit a great ball. I squeaked out a 7-6 first set, using my serve and volley style. As we started the 2nd set, I realized I couldn't put the ball away with the deader balls. His strokes were too good. I decided to let go of the set and save my energy for the 3rd set. I lost it quickly 6-0. We then got new, more lively balls for the 3rd set, which I again won in a close 7-6 set. Using our model:

> *Present State/Problem:* The balls are deader in the second set. It will be difficult for me to put the ball away, given his strong strokes.

> *Desired State/Goal:* Figure out how to give myself the best chance to win this match.

> *Resource:* In a controversial move, I decided to not waste my energy and allowed the 2nd set to go quickly, calculating my best chance was to play at full go for the 3rd set. I would not normally do this, but my sense was that this would be my best chance to win this match. The Resource here is to be Self Accepting of my limits and strengths and do the best I can, focusing on my Possibilities.

In another match, where I was playing in the USTA National 35 Grass Courts against Andy Moffitt, I lost the first set 6-0. My game is suited to grass courts, because my left-handed serve stays so low and wide. Here, though, it turned out Moffitt had a really good low backhand return. So I had to make some kind of adjustment. I decided to change my game plan and serve to his forehand. It turned the match, and I won. Using our model:

> *Present State/Problem:* My plan A strategy of serving to his backhand isn't working.

Desired State/Goal: Find a way to hold serve

Resource: Switch my game plan, and serve to his forehand.

In my first ever national match, I played a really good player and friend from Ohio, Mike Dahm, at the National 35 Indoors in St. Louis. I knew he served, volleyed and moved really well. We had played against each other in doubles. I expected a very tough, close match and that I would need to give it my best. I play my best when I am in a Determined mental state, so staying in this mental state was my performance goal for the match. Doing this, I won in a 3rd set tiebreaker, 7-6.

Present State/Problem: I am in my Determined mental state during the match.

Desired State/Goal: I need to maintain my Determined mental state throughout the match

Resources: Keep my focus on my energy and inner resolve throughout the match by picturing it during each changeover.

I am suggesting your task as a Self Coach is to use this model to organize your experience, being Aware of what is going on NOW, determining the OUTCOME you would like, and then focusing on accessing the RESOURCES that will help you get to your outcome. This will apply to every experience, so it is helpful to get skilled at this. The following chapters will teach you about Perspectives, Mental Skills, Mental States, Tennis Performance Categories (Mental States, Strokes, Game Plan, Physical State, Relationship Issues, Personal/Psychological Issues, etc.) and the Event Management Sequence of pre-match Preparation, during match Adjustments, and post match Review. Using this Self Coaching Experience Organizing Model is helpful whether you are attending to any of the above issues.

So, for example, if you are not in a positive Self Coaching Perspective, you can use this model to select a desired Perspective. If you are not in a positive Mental State, you can use this model to access a more positive

Mental State. You will learn to do this in the following chapters, but understand you use this Self Coaching Experience Organizing Model in each instance.

ADDITIONAL SELF COACHING EXPERIENCE ORGANIZING MODELS

Now let's turn to some other ways to organize our experience so we can manage it effectively. It can help to have some choices. I am going to say a little more about the NLP Outcome Frame and then discuss Gestalt Therapy, Milton Erickson's concept of Utilization, Self Coaching with the Unconscious, and Ernest Rossi's approaches to doing inner work to access inner resources. I find this information to be fascinating and can be very useful, but is not a quick read. You may want to come back to the rest of this chapter after you have read the rest of the book, and when you have time to study this.

VARIATION ON NLP OUTCOME FRAME

Having a model like the NLP Outcome Frame allows you to sort your issues with clarity and direction. I want to add that Robert Dilts, one of the early pioneers in NLP, who worked with co founders Richard Bandler and John Grinder, and continues to be a leader in the field, has added to the NLP Outcome Frame. The enhanced model is called S.C.O.R.E.. The acronym stands for Symptoms, Cause, Outcome, Resources, Effect. Here the Symptoms are your Present/Problem State, with the Cause being what caused the Symptoms. The Effects are what you get from reaching your Outcome. Your Resources can be selected to respond to the Symptoms and the Cause. If you are pressuring yourself to play well with worries about not doing well because you lack confidence (Cause), and this creates a tense mental state (Symptom), you could make an adjustment to your mental state by doing Relaxation skills (responding to the Symptom) and use some combination of Self Coaching Perspectives ("I just need to do what I know and that is doable"; and "focus on my process and not worry about the outcome") which responds to the Cause and Symptoms. It is also useful to know that your outcome helps you achieve certain Effects. If I am a tennis player not confident in my backhand volley, having my confidence in that will give me the opportunity to be more comfortable moving forward in a point. Also, if my level of play improves, I will feel more able to compete well in my matches and future events. It is helpful to know the S.C.O.R.E. Model and keep it in mind, but for quick in the moment processing during a performance or interaction, I like the simplicity of using the NLP Outcome Frame, with my Self Coach working with my Self to achieve outcomes.

Now let's turn to another organizing model.

THE GESTALT CYCLE OF EXPERIENCE

In addition to the NLP practitioner and master practitioner certi-fication programs I participated in, I also completed a 2 year Intensive Training in Gestalt Methods at the Gestalt Institute of Cleveland. The main founder of Gestalt Therapy was Fritz Perls. His wife, Laura Perls, also a practitioner, called Gestalt Therapy an existential, experiential, and experimental approach. It was developed as a reaction to classical psychoanalysis. Instead of focusing on "talking about" and insight, the approach focuses on Awareness and being present in the moment. The idea was to be able to work with someone's process in the moment. By attending to one's Awareness it would be possible to know what was going on with a person, and life would emerge from there. Speaking to healthy process, the goal became to have healthy Contact.

When I trained at the Gestalt Institute of Cleveland, we learned about the Gestalt Cycle of Experience. This model describes a healthy way to move through experience. The Gestalt Cycle of Experience goes like this: First you get Sensation (eg. Experiencing something in the stomach), then have Awareness (eg. That stomach Sensation means I am hungry), then you have Mobilization of Energy (eg. Experience a build up of energy to be able to mobilize), then take Action (eg. Walk to the refrigerator to get an apple), after which you make good quality Contact (eg. Chew the apple well, swallow the parts you want), after which you can Withdraw and Assimilate the experience (eg. Satiated, you are done eating, and able to digest the apple, then ready for the next experience). So it goes: Sensation…..Awareness…..Mobilization of Energy…..Action…..Contact…..Withdrawal and Assimilation. Then ready for the next cycle of experience.

In healthy functioning you move through the Gestalt Cycle of Experience smoothly. Different things can happen, though, which can disrupt moving through the cycle. Do you get overwhelmed or confused by Sensations, and have difficulty getting Awareness? Do you jump from Sensations to Action, bypassing Awareness? Do you overthink things and have trouble moving from Awareness to Mobilization of Energy and Action? Do you tighten up and restrict your ability to make Contact? Do you act but not make good, solid Contact? Are you so busy acting impulsive or being distracted that you miss out on a good connection? Are you fearful of allowing yourself to be fully you, and somehow back away from good Contact? Do you not know when to stop and Withdraw? Do you have trouble reflecting and learning from your experience and moving to the next one? All kinds of things can occur which can disrupt your ability to move through the cycle.

How do you do moving through the Gestalt Cycle of Experience? In tennis, are you able to make sense of what is going on within you and outside of you to come up with an Awareness that can lead you to Mobilize Energy and Action with good Contact? Do your feelings of tension, frustration, discouragement, or anger, as reactions to events in a match, interfere with your ability to be present for each point? In good Contact we are present and fully ourselves when relating in the world. Interestingly, in tennis this also includes making good Contact with our strokes. This is helped by being fully engaged with optimal physical support, focus and presence. Playing tennis, we have the goal of healthy Contact.

I value the understanding of the Gestalt Cycle of Experience as a way of understanding how I or someone else is moving through the cycle to be fully present during a match. I have an additional way of using the Gestalt Therapy model as an organizing model. Let's call it the Gestalt Therapy Concepts Organizing Model.

GESTALT THERAPY CONCEPTS ORGANIZING MODEL

Three concepts that are foundational to Gestalt Therapy are Awareness, Experiment and Contact. Awareness refers to our immediate attention to noticing where we are, noticing our sensations, feelings, behavior, etc.. How could you guide yourself if you were not aware of your feelings, thoughts, interests, values, needs, reactions, symptoms, associations, behavioral patterns, effects on others, etc.. Awareness enables you to identify your needs and helps you make sense of your experience. We can then work with our experience by Experimenting with it. Joseph Zinker, in *Creative Process in Gestalt Therapy,* writes a full explication of how to Experiment with your experience. The ability to maneuver with your experience helps you make needed adjustments.

For example, as I play a tennis match, I may note that I am being too soft with my shot selection, trying to be clever rather than physical. I may notice that when I get a short ball I am tending to try a deft drop shot, but my opponent is quick and running them down. As such, I could experiment with what happens if I decide to punch my volleys, being more aggressive.

Another example is if you are relating with a significant other too impatiently, and finding there is some tension and unpleasantness between the two of you. You could decide to experiment with being more patient. You might address the issue with the other. You might find the relationship begins to turn for the better. You can also experiment with your sensations, to help you build your awareness. When you notice sensations of tightness in your chest and throat, for example, you can exaggerate the tightness as a way if highlighting the way you are holding yourself back from voicing your feelings. You can then move toward healthy Contact with how you want to use your voice.

The idea is that a healthy experience ends in good Contact, a positive meeting of Self and boundary. In the example of being tense about hitting a backhand volley, I can first be Aware of being tense. Then I can notice where and how I tense. I can experiment with letting go of the tension or increasing it. I can discover what happens if I attack the ball rather than tightening when it comes to me. At each step of the way, I am looking for good, healthy Contact, where I fully embrace whatever I am experimenting with. Ultimately I will see if I am able to see the ball and hit the ball solidly with good Contact. After I am done with the Contact and the experience, I can look for the next experience to experience. So, I can cycle through Awareness to Experiment to Contact…to Awareness… to Experiment…to Contact…Notice how similar this is to the NLP Outcome Frame. We can overlay them as we sort our experiences:

NLP:	Present State/Problem	Resources	Desired State/Goal
Gestalt:	Awareness	Experiment	Contact

The NLP Outcome Frame needs Awareness to identify a Present State/Problem, uses Experiments to utilize Resources, and has the Goal/Desired State of making good, healthy Contact. My goal here is to build your toolbox of ways you can Self-Coach your experiences through Organizing Models that make sense to you. Feel free to select what seems useful to you.

MILTON ERICKSON THERAPY CONCEPT: UTILIZATION

My training has also included significant study and training in Ericksonian (Milton Erickson) approaches to hypnosis and psychotherapy. Milton Erickson pioneered a creative, practical approach to working with the conscious and unconscious mind that is called a Utilization approach. I bring it up here to provide you with another option for your Self Coaching.

Utilization refers to the capacity to make use of whatever a person brings to a situation—whether feelings, interests, values, behavioral patterns, etc. I will here share some of his case stories to help demonstrate this. A little boy who couldn't read was referred to Erickson. Erickson determined that the boy was interested in geography. He showed the boy a map and started giving incorrect information about where states and cities were. The boy knew better and started to read to show Erickson where the places were more correctly located. It wasn't long before the boy was reading. Another boy was referred to him for bed-wetting. Erickson realized the boy liked baseball, so talked with the boy about the muscular control involved in opening and closing his glove at the right time in order to catch a baseball, and take the ball out of the glove to be able to throw it. Without having to talk about the bed-wetting at all, which Erickson thought would be shaming, the boy was able to develop his muscular control and get over his problem. (Bill O'Hanlon, in his book, *Taproots,* explains this as a Class of Problems, Class of Solutions model. He says muscular control, in this example, is the issue with bed-wetting, so you can solve the problem by working on muscular control in baseball.).

In another example, an elderly woman was lonely, depressed and suicidal. The only thing she really got joy out of life was her garden. Erickson suggested she look in the paper for events in the town (i.e.

weddings, deaths, etc) and then bring the town's folk flowers from her garden to commemorate their event. It turned out the people really appreciated her thoughtfulness and she ended up cultivating a meaningful social network. In another case, a young woman was depressed and suicidal. Erickson suggested that since she was apt to kill herself anyway, she might as well spend the little money she had to get some nice outfits, so that she would look her best. She had a space between her front teeth, so he suggested she squirt some water at a work employee she liked, after she managed to be with him at the work water fountain. He ended up viewing it as playful, chased her, and they then found they liked each other a lot. They ended up getting married and forming a family together.

In another case, a fellow came into Erickson's office unable to sit down due to being so agitated. Erickson paced his agitation, acknowledging that he couldn't sit down in the office, and encouraged him to walk to one end of the office....then to another end of the office... then to (pause...this side of the office...then...(longer pause)...to this side.... Until the man was slowed up enough to be able to sit down and have a good session. This idea of pacing where you are and then being able to lead to a desired place, can be helpful in your own coaching of yourself. It is called Pacing and Leading. I hope, from these examples, you can see the value of utilizing your own interests, values, reactions, symptoms, etc as you do your self-coaching.

Can you see how you can use Utilization in your own Self Coaching? I often think of it as making the best with what you have. One winter, years ago, I had a pulled hamstring, and it was hard to run. I still wanted to play tennis, but needed to be careful with my movement. I started returning serve close to the service line. Doing this I could be effectively offensive with my return of serve, and was already in position, so didn't need to move much. Of course, I still needed to be careful with my movement. After rotator cuff surgery, my shoulder took time to build strength. So I crafted an overhead drop serve, that is still useful to throw in once in awhile. We utilize what we have.

I like to use the NLP Outcome Frame as a primary Self Coaching Organizing Model, with Utilization being available in terms of thinking of Resources (or Experiments, if you are in the Gestalt Concepts Organizing Model).

SELF COACHING WITH THE UNCONSCIOUS

Just like we have a Self and Self Coach that can work together to help us manage our experience and performance, so do we also have an Unconscious. A lot of people don't seem to utilize the information, wisdom and powers of the unconscious mind optimally. Sigmund Freud made a tremendous contribution when he pioneered how our unconscious mind, our other than conscious mind, is a huge influence on our behavior. Our unconscious communicates with us through our feelings, urges, reactions, slips of the tongue, fantasies and dreams. There is meaning to this and it helps to reveal our inner life and personal psychology. Milton Erickson, was a preeminent psychiatrist of the 20th century, who used hypnosis to help people achieve outcomes beyond what they could do just using the conscious mind. He championed the idea that the Unconscious is a vast, positive, inner resource, harboring our memories, wisdom, and creativity. My Mom, who studied with Theodore Reik, a disciple of Freud, who wrote, *Listening With The Third Ear,* emphasized with me the importance of attending to my reactions, when speaking with people and performing. Timothy Gallwey, with his *Inner Game of Tennis, Inner Tennis,* and other inner game books, highlighted that to play best we need to be able to access the automaticity of our unconscious mind. We focus, we gaze, but we don't *try* to focus. He separated out the conscious self from the unconscious self, calling them self 1 and self 2. My take on all this is that it is important to heed the messages to us from the Unconscious, *in addition* to realizing we can communicate with the Unconscious. I agree with Stephen Gilligan, who in *Generative Trance* acknowledges our conscious self and Unconscious can be in dialogue. I have always thought of it this way. While we can bypass the conscious mind to go on automatic to perform optimally, our conscious mind and Unconscious dialogue for our optimal self management. Sometimes it is very helpful to draw on our unconscious wisdom, especially when our conscious mind is stuck. Let me give you an example.

Years ago, when I was trying to figure out a topic for my dissertation, I was consciously stuck. I had spent a few months reading and pondering what to research, but to no avail. I thought I had given myself enough preparation to come up with something, but I did not have a topic that felt right to me. I decided to ask my Unconscious for help with this. When I went to sleep, I put a pad of paper and pen by my bedside. I asked my inner self to please dream me a dream about what to research for my dissertation. In the middle of the night I had a relevant dream, and while still mostly asleep, wrote on the pad what I was dreaming. I woke up in the morning and knew that I had dreamt something, but couldn't quite remember. So I looked at the pad of paper, and there it was! My Unconscious had come up with an idea of an Interpersonal Life Diagram. The context for this was that in my therapy practice I was getting quick, positive outcomes with clients but a part of me had the sense that I wasn't getting a good enough look at their interpersonal worlds. I wanted to understand them more fully. Seeing this idea, I felt it was a good idea, selected it, and enthusiastically worked on the project. This is an example of my Conscious mind asking my Unconscious for help, and getting a helpful, creative response.

What are some other ways we can access our Unconscious resources? Going inside our minds to pause and reflect can allow us to do creative inner work that helps us discover things.

ROSSI'S FOUR STAGE CREATIVE PROCESS

Ernest Rossi was a long time student, collaborator and historian of Milton Erickson, who went on to develop his own way of practicing. He is not the creator of the Four Stage Creative Process, but used it as an organizing model in his work. He wrote about it in several books and papers, one of which is *The Psychobiology of Gene Expression*. This model is emphasizing that it is helpful to go inside your mind to allow your inner self to reflect, allowing unconscious wisdom and creativity to explore and come up with ideas. Here it is:

1. **Stage 1:** Initiation: You begin by gathering information and selecting a topic.

2. **Stage 2:** Incubation: In this stage your mind frees up to explore and make connections about the topic. Your task is to allow your inner mind to continue processing until you experience some understanding. It is important to continue the process as you begin to feel excited or uncomfortable, so that your inner mind can do it's exploring and problem solving. A tendency otherwise may be to stop the process if uncomfortable, but then you don't get to the next stage.

3. **Stage 3:** Illumination: This stage is where you get some understanding or insight that has emerged from your exploring.

4. **Stage 4:** Implementation: In this stage your Conscious mind can turn the discoveries of the inner mind into some practical gains. You can make sense of what you have come up with and decide whether and how your new understanding can make a difference in your life. This can involve some plans and actions.

We can view my story about figuring out my dissertation topic as an example of using the 4 stage creative process:

1. **Stage 1:** Consciously exploring a variety of possibilities for selecting a research topic. Gathering information.

2. **Stage 2:** Self asking Inner Self (Unconscious) to dream a dream about a possible topic. While half asleep writing down a dreamed up idea.

3. **Stage 3:** Aha experience. Waking up and realizing I had dreamed a dream that felt relevant to me.

4. **Stage 4:** Selecting the dream as my dissertation topic. Making a plan for following up with the research topic idea. Writing my dissertation.

So, as a way of guiding yourself you can select a topic where you want to have access to your inner wisdom. For example, you can ask yourself how you can improve your tennis game, and be receptive to forthcoming ideas. You don't have to do this in a dream. You can also go inside your mind to pause and reflect. Sometimes you may be surprised by the answers you get, sometimes discovering something you had not thought about. At other times you may get support for what you thought you needed.

ROSSI'S IDEOMOTOR APPROACH

One specific way to pause and reflect to get information and answers you are looking for is to use ideomotor techniques. Ideo-motor refers to ideas affecting movement. David Cheek wrote a seminal book, *Hypnosis: The Application of Ideomotor Techniques.* Here, though, I am speaking more to the approach Ernest Rossi taught about using ideomotor techniques. He emphasized the idea of getting inner answers through hand movements. I especially like his books, *The Symptom Path of Enlightenment, The Psychobiology of Gene Expression,* and co-authored with Richard Hill, *Mirroring Hands.* It takes training and experience to learn how to use Rossi's ideomotor approach (he also called it a mirroring hands approach), but I want to provide you with an example as an introduction to this process.

Here is one example of how you can have your Self and Unconscious work together to get some inner answers:

You can hold your hands facing each other, in front of you a few inches apart, and a couple feet from your lap. Hold your hands close enough so that you can feel the energy and heat from your hands. We are looking to build a learning about automatic movement with the hands, so we can set up a signal system and ask ourselves yes and no questions, waiting for our inner self to answer automatically. So, you might suggest that if the answer is yes, the hands will move closer to each other, while if the answer is no, those hands may drift apart. You can then ask a person questions like "what food do you like a lot", and allow those hands to move towards each other on their own to indicate what is true for you. Or " what food do you not like", and allow those hands to drift apart to indicate you don't like that food.

Of course, you could ask questions about books, movies, sports teams, etc., instead of food. When a person can have their hands moving all by themselves (not just consciously moving them), then you can begin asking questions of personal relevance to them, to get some inner ideas and answers. A problem solving way to do this is to say "allow one hand to drift down slowly to your lap while you explore how you can do better in your tennis matches (or insert any other question of interest—how can you improve your backhand; how can you handle your emotions better on the court, etc.). As the one hand drifts closer to your lap, you can then say, "now allow the other hand to drift down as you explore what you can do to apply the ideas you have been discovering". Once your hands reach your lap, or you feel ready, you can take a few moments to consider what you have discovered. Sometimes you will get some novel ideas that show you a way you have not really been considering. At other times you may just get support for the ideas you have already been consciously considering. There is something special, however, about experiencing potential ideas as coming from within.

Ideomotor communicating is a way to have a communication between your Self and Inner Self (Unconscious). I do caution you, however, to consult a therapist if you want to do this work with heavy personal issues. Also, don't necessarily take as gospel what you are receiving when you do the inner work. Your Self still needs to consider the viability, judiciousness and usefulness of the ideas received. This is a collaboration between your Self and Unconscious. I want to add that in addition to the value of the collaboration between the Self and the Unconscious, there is value in learning the automatic responses you get to learn with the hand movements. This helps you learn to trust your inner self for responding when you play tennis. When we play we want to be able to trust our strokes with Confidence and Relaxation, and be able to hit freely without conscious interference. We can select how we want to be play but then we want to allow ourselves to flow freely. We will do more work on accessing Mental States for playing well in our Mental State and Mental Skills training chapters.

What questions or communication would you like with your inner self right now? Are you wondering how you can improve your tennis game, and what is most important to work on? Are you wondering what is most important to help your mental game? Or how you can get over an injury? You can explore the issue, and you can do problem solving. Whatever you are interested in exploring, how about taking the time to pause and reflect, going inside to discover how your inner wisdom can support and help you.

SUMMARY AND IMPORTANCE OF USING AN EXPERIENCE ORGANIZING MODEL

As a way to do effective Self Coaching we have been exploring Experience Organizing Models for sorting our experience, and have added ways to communicate with our Inner Self as a help to understanding ourselves and engage in positive problem solving. Using a model like the NLP Outcome Frame or Gestalt Therapy Concepts Experience Organizing Model allows us to focus on being aware of the present and oriented towards moving towards our desired outcomes. When you miss a shot, you focus on fixing it rather than criticizing yourself or being discouraged. If you are not physically warmed up you focus on how to get more warmed up rather than lamenting your stiffness. Understanding Utilization you use what you have in terms of your available resources. Having trouble with your topspin forehand? There are things you can do to help connect to your topspin forehand, such as imaging the way you hit it when you hit it well, but if still struggling you can make effective utilization of your slice forehand or lobbing and drop shots. If consciously stuck, you have the possibility of turning to your Inner Self to get help from your Unconscious to help understand and problem solve. Not sure how to improve your serve? You can go inside your mind and ask your Inner Self for improvement ideas. You can pause and reflect, use ideomotor methods, attend to images you get, or listen to messages in your dreams. All the above shows you how you can working positively with your ongoing experience. This is an important part of your Self-Coaching.

Now we will turn to positive Perspectives we can draw on to put ourselves in a positive frame of mind and attitude while playing tennis and living life.

CHAPTER 4

Self Coaching Perspectives

The Self Coaching (SC) Perspectives set the frame or bigger picture around which we are performing. There are certain useful ways of thinking that help us orient to performing in a way that enhances our experience, facilitates our functioning, and helps us to be the person we want to be while performing. These wise SC Perspectives help us with our 3 Dimensional Self Coaching Functions of: Self Support, Self Activation and Self Direction. Here I am sharing with you a menu of wise perspectives you can choose from when preparing for a performance, playing, and reviewing a performance. This is not a complete list, in that you can continue to add items. I share them with you so you will have clear options to draw from when playing tennis or engaging in other life events and relationships. I want you to feel like you have the tools to Self Coach well. Knowing, understanding and using these SC Perspectives is an important part of your tool bag for Self Coaching.

LIST OF SELF COACHING PERSPECTIVES

1. Learning Frame
2. Opportunity Frame
3. Challenge vs Threat Frame
4. Commit to Staying in a Good Mood
5. Self Acceptance
6. Other Acceptance
7. Curiosity Frame

8. Possibility vs Probability Perspectives

9. Focus on the Process, Don't worry about the Outcome

10. Do What You Know

11. Focus on you Performance Keys

12. In Training

13. Self Connection

Learning Frame: One way to be kind to ourselves is to be in the Learning Frame. When a child learns to walk, tie her shoes, or ride a bike, she is typically focused on learning, working at it as long as it takes, with positive focus. In the Learning Frame, we are interested in improving and developing, and patient about how long this takes. As a musical composer, I will sometimes think of a line in the left hand with an overlay in the right hand that I can't play right away together with the left hand. I don't know how long it will take my brain to create the neuronal connections, but I know to work at it until I get it. That seems better than criticizing myself impatiently for not being able to play it right away. Did you hear about a person who got a dog, and then wanted to train it to fetch her newspaper in the morning? She pointed to the paper at the door and said "ok, bring it to me now." The dog picked up the paper, chewed it to shreds and dropped it at her feet. To teach the dog a lesson, she threw the dog out the window. I grew up on the 9th floor of an apartment in Manhattan in New York City. Thankfully, this woman lived in a house in the suburbs and they were on the first floor. She yelled at the dog, and said "now tomorrow, get it right!" The next day, she nicely said to the dog, "let's get it right this time. Now bring me the paper." The dog brought her the paper, tearing it up again as he dropped it at her feet. Then the dog jumped out the window. So, as you see, when we criticize and berate ourselves, calling ourselves names for being slow or stupid, we actually learn the wrong lesson. In the Learning Frame we give ourselves whatever time we need accepting it takes us as long as it takes us.

Applying this to tennis, in the Learning Frame, you can emphasize with yourself that you are playing to improve. When you miss a shot, you can discover what you need to work on with stroke technique. It is ok not to have it developed yet. You are working on it. Similarly, if you hit the wrong shot, you can examine ways to improve your game plan. When your mental state goes awry, you can work on how to manage your mental state. When in the Learning Frame, you are allowing yourself time to develop, so are less self critical.

Opportunity Frame: We all face adversity and disappointment in our life. It will help us be less depressive if we explore the opportunity in each situation. Leslie Bandler, one of the early pioneers of NLP, told a story of having lost a job. In trying to be helpful in a social work counseling type position she had gone out with a person into the community to help her function. Her employer disapproved of her attempt to help outside the office, and fired her. She was initially taken aback, but then using the Opportunity Frame, she explored new chances to help people, and ended up being involved in the development of Neuro-Linguistic Programming. My son, Cole, teaches tennis in L.A.. For his first several years he worked at a public park facility. He did a fantastic job, and stayed with it, appreciating that it was a stable job. At a certain point, though, new management came to run the place, and they decided to make his job even less lucrative. Cole quit the job, which was scary, because it was his livelihood, but he also trusted he could find opportunities in the community. He was able to find a way to teach private lessons and do clinics in the community in a way that worked out even better to him. He contacted a friend, who was starting a tennis teaching community, and wanted to involve Cole in the work. This provided him with additional tennis client referrals and places to teach.

If I get sick or injured and can't play one of my tennis events, I similarly look for ways to make the best of a difficult situation. In 2007 I was diagnosed with hairy cell leukemia. Thankfully, this is a treatable form of leukemia. I needed chemo, and needed post chemo surgery for infections. While recovering, I did what I could to get back in shape. I was thankful for the opportunity to heal and the opportunity to rehab. Three months after the surgery, my son and I won a national father-son tournament. We may have loss and adversity to process, but it still helps us to look for the opportunities that arise in each situation. That will help us be less depressive in our approach to life.

In terms of your tennis and life, what adversity or disappointments are you dealing with, where you could explore your opportunities? Do you have an injury, where you have the opportunity to get enthusiastically involved in your rehab so that you can come back even stronger than before? Are you not able to go to an event, but can use the time to train extra or spend some needed time on another project or relationship? By the way, let's not think we need to wait for adversity to select the Opportunity Frame. When things are going fine, we can also explore our opportunities to develop and enhance ourselves.

Challenge vs Threat Frame: We can approach an event as if it is a challenge or a threat. As a challenge, we are eager to perform and show what we can do. Ever study hard for a test in school, and be eager to take the test? If that has happened to you, you know you are motivated and excited, confident and eager to perform. Conversely, when it feels like a threat to perform, you are fearful of being found out as an imposter, who is not as good a performer as people thought. In this case, performing/playing can feel like a threat to one's identity. As an approach to performing, it helps to think in terms of doing what one knows how to do, not worrying about whether that is good enough for others or not. When in the Challenge Frame, excitement is positive energy. In the Threat Frame, excitement is experienced as anxiety, and a lot of relaxation skills work is needed. Fritz Perls, the founder of Gestalt Therapy, said the difference between excitement and anxiety is that in excitement you provide more self support from your breathing. As an approach to performing, it seems best if you can put yourself in a framework of looking forward to the challenge. In tennis, do you find it more pressure to play someone better than you, at your level, or below your level? Do you worry about losing, or losing your ranking? Can you find the challenge in playing whoever it is? It's about challenging yourself to play at your best level regardless who you play.

Healthy Frame: Most of us have a good model of what it means to be a healthy person in a situation. We seem to understand the positive character traits of being honest, responsible, hard working, mature, empathic, thoughtful, etc. The field of positive psychology has helped to define and study these character strengths. It is in our best interests and the interests of those around us if we can orient to the idea of "being a good person." If we orient to the Healthy Frame, we will be more apt to behave in a way we feel good about. When I was in the 6th grade, at P.S.6 in Manhattan, my mother took me to get allergy shots every Wednesday. She was a successful, hard working psychoanalyst in the city, but took off work to go to the doctor. The doctor was across the street from Bloomingdales. My mother often asked if we could stop there, so she could get a few things. She didn't have other times she could get away to do that, because her schedule was full. I didn't create a big commotion, but I usually was impatient, wanting to go play ball of some kind after school and my allergy shot. My mom was a quick decision maker, stopping at just a couple of counters to purchase some things.

One day, after my allergy shot, I asked her if she wanted to go to Bloomingdales. She said "that would be lovely." She stopped at the first counter and got something. I asked her if she wanted to go to the other counter. She said "that would be great. Thank you". When she was done with that, I asked her if she needed to stop at another counter. She then said, "OK. It's wonderful you are being so patient about me getting some things, but what's up?" I said I had just found out in school I had gotten into a special program where I would be skipping a grade in school, actually doing 7th, 8th, and 9th grades in two years. I figured if I was selected to be in that program it was time for me to be more mature. We tend to have a good idea of what it means to be healthy, but our task is to use that model. This is so simple, but people need to use the Healthy Frame more. How can you be in the Healthy Frame in tennis and life? Rather than play frustrated, anxious or angry about missing shots or being behind in a match, you might stay composed, doing the best you can in each point.

Maintaining a positive attitude will tend to be the healthy or mature thing to do. I've had several matches in singles and doubles, where I lost the first set 6-0, and then turned the match around and won. Rather than get upset or discouraged, I kept interested in what I could do to stay present in the match and do what I could. I think it is healthy and mature to focus on doing the best you can in any given moment, not letting things upset or distract you.

Commit to Staying in Good Mood: This is setting the frame with Enjoyment. We often participate in performances doing activities we want and like to do. The musician likes music and wants to express that music. The tennis player enjoys tennis and the chance to compete. Yet things can happen that take the joy away. A musician can have trouble with her instrument or be upset about making a mistake. A tennis player can also get distracted by a bad call or upset by an errant shot. If the Frame we set is to Stay in a Good Mood, we are more likely to let adversity just roll off of us. This helps us be more resilient. In 2010, I was the player captain of a 4 player team representing the United States in the ITF 60&over World Team Championships played in Antalya, Turkey. As player captain I helped with our arrangements, scheduled our team practices, and conferred with the players while being responsible for setting the lineup for each match. As a player, I was the doubles specialist on the team, with the format being two singles and a doubles match against other countries. The night before the first match, I had a dream in which I heard the song, "When You're Smiling". I don't usually think of this song, so it occurred to me there was meaning to this dream. This was a message from my unconscious.

As I interpreted it, the dream was telling me to Stay in a Good Mood throughout the event. This became important for me. There was some rain and I had to do extra walking to the playing venue to get our changing schedule information. This would normally not be a problem, but I was having some hip pain walking. Seven months later I actually got a hip replacement. Given the dream, though, I stayed in good spirits. Our team reached the finals, against the defending champion team from Spain. There was some rain before the finals and a little work was needed with the court that delayed things. The match began and Brian Cheney, playing #2 singles, played brilliantly and won his match. Larry Turville then lost at #1 singles to a terrific player. He was upset about losing the match, but mustered up his energy to play doubles with me in the deciding match. Our doubles match turned out to be a tough one. We split the first two sets, and were down a break in the 3rd set, and break point down to go down a second break. In good spirits, I walked slowly up to Larry and said, "Let's play one point at a time." We ended up holding serve, breaking back and going to a 3rd set tie-breaker. We were the last of the age groups to still be playing since it was a long match. We were playing under dim lights, and the players from the other age group teams gathered around to cheer before the trophy presentations. In a thrilling finish, we won the tie-breaker. I still credit setting the Frame of Staying in a Good Mood, from the When You're Smiling dream, as a big part of handling the event successfully.

Self Acceptance: Self Acceptance is the basis for a number of the Self Coaching Perspectives. You can't have a Learning Frame, for example, without being patient about your rate of learning, which is based on self acceptance. Being in a Healthy Frame will include being Self Accepting, since being healthy includes accepting where you are at this moment. Given it's importance, it makes sense to commit to Self Acceptance as a Self Coaching Perspective. As I enter an event, whether it is a tennis match, musical performance or some other performance, it seems like a good idea to be Self Accepting. That means I set the frame of being compassionate about where I am. That way I am more apt to flow with mistakes I make or difficulties I run into. The "that's ok" response is a good way to behaviorally flow with what happens. If a musician makes an error, or a tennis player misses a shot, it works well to automatically say, "that's ok" to oneself. Following that you can quickly decode what went wrong so you can fix it, or at least make the best of the circumstance.

Do you tend to be self critical, or are you Self Accepting about your mistakes, limits, deficits, and difficulties? Being Self Accepting is you being kind and self compassionate, which enables you to have a positive experience, as you decide how to best handle things in the moment. I have had 2 USTA national doubles events, where I played with a herniated disc in my back and still won. Being Self Accepting, I accepted the limits of my movement. I could serve, return and volley, but couldn't move much without risking further harm. I had to set my brain to include my limited movement. In one of the events, Phil Landauer and I were playing in the USTA national 40 Indoors in Kansas City. Phil understood my situation and we played with the idea of doing the best we could with what we had. Wouldn't you know, I hit a topspin lob during the match, and one of our opponents hurt his back going for it. He had more trouble playing with the new injury, and Phil and I won.

Other Acceptance: Being compassionate with others, as with being compassionate with oneself, is important to being a good person while performing, and important to being able to maintain one's positive mental state even when others do things that we do not prefer. My task when performing is to maintain my focus and energy regardless of what happens. If I get angry, frustrated and disappointed readily with others' behaviors, I will likely find my mental state and performance level get disrupted. Being accepting of others is easiest when we are empathic of them. Being empathic and accepting of others doesn't mean we like or agree with what they did or are doing. Rather, it suggests you accept that they have a right to being different, or that anyone can make a mistake. If you are a person that spends a lot of time with a disrupted mental state because you are upset with others, you might want to select Other Acceptance as a Self Coaching Perspective for an event. The "that's ok" response is useful here, too. It helps if we can flow with an opponent's bad calls, perceived official's errors, or other adversity that occurs during a performance. Saying "that's ok" right away helps you not overreact, after which you can problem solve what to do next.

Curiosity Frame: Feelings are information. When we have a feeling, symptom, or reaction of some kind it helps to be curious about what the message is telling us. Let us also be curious when we have performance issues of any kind. Performance disruptions can occur for a variety of reasons. The basketball player, for example, can drift too much and break technique on a jump shot (Performance Skill issue) , or lose motivation when ahead and not play with enough energy on defense (Mental State issue), or struggle moving due to stepping on someone's foot (Physical State issue), or get beaten by guarding someone to their left when they only tend to move right (Strategy issue). Welcoming the message for its information value, it is more useful to decode and problem solve what is going on, rather than waste our energy criticizing ourselves or someone else, or lamenting our plight. That way we can make adjustments in our performance skill, mental state, physical state, or game plan, or whatever category needs attention.

Possibility vs Probability Perspectives: It is not unusual to calculate the odds of a performance ahead of time. A problem with probability thinking, however, is if we determine the opponent is a better player, or the challenge of the performance is too difficult, we can get defeatist in attitude and give less than our best in the performance. When I was in my mid 30's I played an open tennis tournament against a player who just a couple of weeks before had been the top player in the Mid American Conference, Marty Reist. Playing at Ball State, he had been the best player at #1 singles in the conference. When we warmed up, I noticed he had no weakness in his game. He was a lefty, young, quick, and strong with excellent serve, strokes and volleys. My impression was he had advantages over me as a player, but there still was a Possibility I could compete with him in the match. We were playing on a fast, indoor court. I thought the surface might help me hold serve. My hope was my serve and volley game would be effective on that surface. My prognostications held true. He played very solid and stable, through the first set, and held serve all the way through the set. It wasn't easy, but on the surface it turned out I could hold serve, too. My first volley could do enough that I had a way to finish points, so I also held serve throughout the first set. We went to a tie-breaker. I took a chance and moved forward on some returns in the tie-breaker, and won it. The second set proved identical, so I won the match 7-6, 7-6. The Probability was that he would win the match, but what proved helpful was realizing my Possibility.

Focus on the Process, Don't worry about the Outcome: This perspective is the best way to take pressure off of ourselves, and free up to perform our best. It is all too common to worry about making a mistake and losing or having a bad performance. When you focus on the process, rather than be concerned about a negative outcome, we focus on how we want to perform. Tuning in to how you want to play, you focus on hitting the tennis ball with a positive mental state, using your good technique, and using your decided game plan. Is that good enough to win? I don't know, but it maximizes my chances of doing the best I can. I once worked with an ice hockey player who was having an excellent year but started pressuring himself about the outcome of scoring a lot of goals. He had gone into a brief slump. I asked him what his process had been when he had been playing well. Indeed, rather than pressuring himself to score goals, he had been seeing the whole rink better, and had been more into the flow of the game. He returned to the process, and the slump lifted. He started getting more assists and then the goals came by being in the process of the flow of the game.

Do What you Know: It can help you take pressure off yourself if you realize your task is just to do what you know. Some people think they need to be better than they are, and pressure themselves to play at a level beyond their current capability. They compare themselves to others unfavorably, and then pressure and criticize themselves. It is fine to train to improve, but let's do the doable: focus on doing what you know. If you learn a new piece of music fairly well, but know you can't quite play it to tempo yet, you are wise to do what you know at your recital. If you can communicate the mood and atmosphere of the piece well, but have some difficult runs not learned perfectly yet, your task may be to keep true to the atmosphere of the piece while faking your way a bit through those unpolished sections. Knowing what you don't know is helpful so you can practice improving, but at performance time it helps to do what you know. This harkens back to our Self Acceptance perspective. We accept where we are. Doing What You Know helps you stay Confident. You can be confident in what you know, even if the musical piece isn't fully mastered yet.

Focus on your Performance Keys: One way to know how to Focus on your Process is to identify and use your Performance Keys. My best example of this occurred when I played in the USTA 35&over National Grass Courts in Newport, Rhode Island, at the International Tennis Hall of Fame courts in 1985. I usually played singles and doubles at that time, but my doubles partner for the event got hurt. I was then in the situation of only playing singles and there being no backdraw. So if I lost I would be done with the tournament. I usually flew to events like this but for some reason my wife, Rayna, and I had driven to the event from Columbus, Ohio. I was playing a player of equal ability in the first round. It had rained so the ball was skidding a lot on the grass. I won the first set. He won the second. In the third set he went up a break, to go up 2-0. At that point I realized it was certainly possible I would lose the match, and need to drive home after just one match. Since the court was playing with an extra low bounce, it was hard to break serve. It is at that point that I decided on using my Performance Keys. When I served I would serve and volley and make sure I got to at least the service line on each serve. I let go of the Outcome by saying to myself I would accept any hit or miss on the volley as long as I hustled and got good court position. When I returned I said to myself I would get a hop in as my opponent served, and then move forward, doing my best to get to the service line for my second shot. Focusing on my Performance Keys made all the difference. I won the next 6 games in a row, winning the third set 6-2, and winning the match! Keeping my keys in mind, I won a few more matches against excellent players, and ended up being ranked #8 in the country in singles. That was an example of a playing Strategy Performance Key. We can identify Performance Keys in each of the Self Coaching Performance Categories (Mental State, Performance Skill, etc.), or just select one or two like in the example above. When we select a Perspective for the event (e.g. Commit to Staying in a Good Mood, or be in a Learning Frame) that is also an example of identifying a Performance Key for the match.

In Training: Thinking of yourself as perennially "In Training" will help you stay in shape and continue to improve. If you keep mindful that you are "in training" you will tend to make better choices about practicing, exercising, eating, or whatever, based on what you are in training for. It will also mean if you temporarily sway from your discipline of training, which could be reframed as taking a break, you will return to training, rather than thinking all is lost and you are off the training program. For example, if you are trying to get in better shape by eating healthy and exercising, but you have a weekend where you go off your program while you celebrate a family function, you can think of yourself as in training and return to your in training program as soon as the family function is over. By being mindful, some people even make sure they get some practicing time in even during family functions or events with friends. You might wake up early and find a practice room for your music, or go for a run or go to the gym if an athlete, or you might make healthy food choices when it would be tempting to overeat. Taking a break from practicing or working out is important to build in and can be rejuvenating, while preventing overuse injuries, but it is important to think of this within the context of being "in training."

Self Connection: Working with your inner, unconscious resources: I assume we have a conscious mind and an unconscious mind. I believe too many people don't make use of their unconscious, inner resources. I am including this here in the list of Self Coaching Perspectives, so you will be reminded of this as you go through your menu of SC Perspectives. I view our dreams, feelings, reactions and symptoms as messages telling us what is going on within us. The "When You're Smiling" dream I wrote about above in the Commit to Staying in a Good Mood SC Perspective is an example of how helpful it can be to pay attention to communications from within. I believe it is important to understand that the messages we get from a dream or from doing hypnotic inner work can be extra meaningful. If I had simply told myself to smile through the world championships event in Turkey in 2010, it wouldn't have resonated as meaningfully as did the dream. Our conscious mind and unconscious mind can work together to help us reach our desired outcomes. My Mom, psychoanalyst and co-author of How To Be Your Own Best Friend, taught me well about this. She often spoke with me about listening to one's own reactions and associations, and appreciating the messages we get from within in the form of ideas that pop up, dreams or images. She had been a favored student of Theodore Reik, author of Listening With The Third Ear, who trained with Sigmund Freud.

Stephen Gilligan writes wisely about the cooperation and communication between the conscious mind and unconscious mind in his book, Generative Trance. I can share a personal example again of doing this. When I was working on my dissertation in Counseling Psychology at The Ohio State University years ago, I had difficulty coming up with a topic. I was doing a lot of reading and thinking to find a topic, but I couldn't seem to find something I felt good about. Months went by. I finally told myself I had done enough reading and thinking to come up with a topic, but my conscious mind couldn't think of anything. I took a pad and pen and put it by my bedside. Then, speaking to my unconscious, I said to my inner self, "Please dream me a dream of my dissertation topic tonight". I had never done this in this way before, but I felt ready. That night, while dreaming, an idea emerged. I picked up the pen and wrote down what I was dreaming. When I woke up in the morning, I didn't remember what I had dreamed, but I did recall I had written down my dream during the night. I looked at it, and then said to myself, "That's my dissertation topic!" I had been doing quick therapy work with my clients. My unconscious had realized I might be missing the client's interpersonal context to some extent by grasping quickly onto helping people get their outcomes. So the dream was about eliciting a person's interpersonal life diagram so that I could understand that context better. My conscious mind had no idea

I would be dreaming that, but upon awakening realized "this is it!" I never minded the arduous work of the dissertation because the topic came to me in such a meaningful way.

Ernest Rossi details his ideomotor approach to working with your inner self in several of his books, including *The Symptom Path to Enlightenment* and *The Psychobiology of Gene Expression*. I won't detail his approach here, but, as examples, he has ways we can set up a yes-no signal system and ask questions with automatic arm and hand responses as answers from within, or allows hand polarity parts to explore issues, or encourages a person to track the path of their symptoms across sensations, feelings, memories, physical symptoms, and images as we get messages from within. Remember, the messages we get when working with our inner self tend to feel extra meaningful, just like when we get messages in a dream. I used some of his ideas to help my students in the Music Performance Enhancement classes I taught at Ohio State University. In the follow up, advanced class we would sometimes do some self hypnosis training. The students learned to explore their music performance issues at a deeper level of self connection, and learned to check with their inner self about their readiness to perform. The idea is that we perform best when we have a positive self connection.

The above Self Coaching Perspectives provide us with a menu of wise Perspectives to draw on when involved in a performance. It would be unfair to ask you to be an effective Self Coach without providing you with an idea about the kinds of Self Coaching Perspectives that are useful and enable you to have a positive frame of mind. These Self Coaching Perspectives are helpful wherever you are in the Event Management Sequence, whether Preparing, Adjusting during play, or Reviewing your playing. In the PAR Approach to Preparing to play, for example, discussed in another chapter, we use an organizing model, like the NLP Outcome Frame Model, to determine where we are, how we would like to play, and how to get there. Knowing how we want to play, we prepare by selecting the wise SC Perspectives we want to keep in mind as we perform, as our context. These wise SC Perspectives, combined with our Mental Skills and Mental States, constitute Resources that ready us to perform well, both in tennis, and in any other life ventures. The list above provides you with a varied host of perspectives to use, but feel free to add to the list.

Before we move on to the next chapter, I want to make sure you understand how to use the Perspectives:

HOW TO SELECT A SELF COACHING PERSPECTIVE

Now that you know a host of Self Coaching Perspectives, how do you select a Perspective to keep in mind while playing? It is simple. Just think about what frame of mind will help you play better. If I have been upset about missing shots, being in a Learning Frame can help me be less frustrated about misses, as I give myself the time to play and learn. Similarly, Focusing On My Process, Not Worrying About The Outcome, will allow me to play with a positive process (eg. staying with good technique on shot; focusing on good court positioning; going for my shot; following my game plan; staying in a desired mental state), letting go of worrying about the outcome of any shot or the score. If I am playing a terrific player, who seems to have playing advantages over me, adopting the Possibility Frame will help me focus on finding ways to be effective against this player. Rather than be discouraged by how good they are, I can be curious and look for my possibilities. My opponent may have better strokes than I do, but how does he do if I hit high loopy balls to his backhand, or rush him by returning serve from close in and coming to net? If I am playing a good player, who I feel like I am "supposed to beat", I may worry about how losing could hurt my ranking. In that case, it may be wise to put myself in a Challenge Frame vs being in a Threat Frame. Here, I would respect my opponent and focus on the Challenge of eagerly giving my best in the match. I would probably combine this with the Focus On My Process perspective. If I am slightly injured, but still playing, I can select the Self Acceptance perspective. Here I do what I can do, without further injuring myself. The examples are endless, but the idea is that you select whatever Self Coaching Perspectives will enable you to have the experience you want on the court, play the way you want, be the person you want to be, and develop the way you want.

BEING IN A FRAME OF MIND

What does it mean to be playing within a Self Coaching Perspective? It means to keep the wisdom of the Perspective in mind as a context as you play. If LeBron James misses a shot, but has the context of knowing he is a great player and scorer, missing that shot doesn't phase him. He still knows he is a good scorer and has confidence in his next shot. When you take a child to the grocery store, you may prepare them with the idea we are just running in for milk and not staying to browse the aisles. This may help prepare the child, who is then less likely to rant about wanting a host of things. If I want to react in a Healthy Frame in my match, I set that as a goal and keep that in mind as things occur in a match. If I miss a shot, instead of getting frustrated or discouraged, I do what a person in a Healthy Frame does. To me that means being Self Accepting about the miss, and Curious about how to make whatever adjustment will help me to play the next point. If my doubles partner is struggling, being in a Healthy Frame, I support my partner rather than criticize. Our task, then, is to keep the selected Perspective in the back of our mind as the context for our play. This requires that we understand the Perspective and what being in it entails. In the Learning Frame, for example, I am truly being patient with myself, giving myself a chance to practice and learn. If events occur and you seem to be getting upset and losing the Perspective, you can remind yourself about being in the frame of mind you want, and re-access the Perspective. This is based on the understanding that we can select a positive Perspective context that will help us function. This is Self Coaching.

CHAPTER 5

Mental Skills Training

Mental Skills are an important component of our Self Coaching. We can learn to use our Sensory Resources, that is, our visual, auditory and kinesthetic resources, to affect and manage our experience. For example, how we talk with ourselves can soothe us, activate and guide us, or scare us, upset us and discourage us. We can not only select the content of what we say, but also vary our voice tempo, tone, and timbre to help reach our outcomes. We are not just a recipient of our self talk; we are also the initiators. So we need to keep that in mind as we talk with ourselves. Similarly, we can image things that help facilitate our experience and performance positively or negatively. We can also vary how we picture things. We can see ourselves out there, or we can image from our own eyes. We can vary the size, colors, and perspective of what we picture to help us. Kinesthetically, we can work with our breathing, muscles, and movement/behavior. In all of these examples, we are learning to be in charge of our experience.

In this chapter we are going to teach Mental Skills through Relaxation skills training. You will learn a host of skills, using your sensory resources, to enter a state of Relaxation. Before I show you this host of skills, I will show you the D-E-E-P approach to Relaxation I developed to help you best learn the skills. This approach will also help you see that we can all benefit from these skills. Since they are skills, I hope you will practice them so that you can develop your ability to use them. In addition to the Relaxation skills training, you will learn some protective devices that can help you not be overstressed and bothered. In the next chapter we will do Mental State Training, which will use mental skills to enter a variety of mental states.

THE D-E-E-P APPROACH TO SELF COACHING AND MENTAL SKILLS TRAINING

I would like you to learn a host of essential Mental Skills in order to be the best Self Coach you can be. So that you can experience the mental skills "deeply", I have come up with an acronym: D = Discrete; E = Effect; E = Everyone; P = Practice. These are fundamental principles that will help you fully experience the Self Coaching resources. Let me now explain each component of the D-E-E-P Approach.

D = Discrete: It is easier to learn something if you keep it simple and not overloaded with information. When I first learned about Relaxation skills, I recall breathing, muscles, images and sounds all being combined in a multifaceted texture. If provided to me by someone else, I could get into the experience of it, but it was too much for me to provide by myself. On the other hand, I could learn each element—breathing calmly, letting go of muscles, images—separately, and then easily provide them for myself. Once each element is learned separately, meaning discretely, you can later combine them how you wish, and it then isn't an overload of information. This works for the host of Relaxation Skills you can learn.

E = Effect: We want our Self Coaching tools to work. Sometimes, though, people use the tools without really experiencing them. I can exhale, and not really relax, or I can really become aware of letting go on the exhale, fully experiencing the richness of inner calm. The Mental Skills really work, but they work by you generating an authentic inner experience—by doing them to Effect. Doing the Mental Skills to Effect will help you utilize them as resources. That said, you can have preferences, preferring certain tools over others, or certain tools to use at certain times. When you use what you select, make sure you do them to Effect.

E = Everyone: Mental Skills work for everyone. I remember some people saying "relaxation doesn't work for me". What they were saying is a particular muscle relaxation skill or breathing focus didn't feel good to them or help them. There are, however, myriad ways to do a skill, and myriad other ways to achieve inner calm. Inner calm is good for Everyone. You just need to discover what works well for you and then provide it for yourself to Effect.

P= Practice: Mental Skills are things to learn. As such, to cultivate Mental Skills it is important to Practice them. If you want to learn a tennis backhand, or how to play the piano, you have to practice the skills. To be good at applying the Mental Skills you need to Practice them. You can mentally rehearse them daily, each one discretely, and you can mentally rehearse them in different life situations. You can then actually use them as you do each life event. That way the Mental Skills become part of your life.

I encourage you to employ the principles of the D-E-E-P Approach as you approach learning how to be your own best Self Coach.

SELF COACHING TOOLS: MENTAL SKILLS TRAINING

Introduction: Below are listed an array of mental skills you can draw on to improve your mental state. The skills are organized by your senses; i.e. Feeling (Kinesthetic), Seeing and Hearing. Organizing them in this way makes it easy to remember and code them for practical use. While you can certainly use these skills while you take 20 minute rejuvenation breaks, you can also use these skills immediately in the moment to access a desired state or shift your state. I assume you function best when in an optimal mental state. The more you practice these skills, the better you can get at being able to work with your mental states. As you try these skills out you may find you have certain preferences. Feel free to use whichever skills you like, and in whatever ways work for you. Please do not feel constrained by the specific procedure I demonstrate for each skill. You may want to experiment with how to creatively tailor the skills to suit you. As you work on accessing a state of inner calm, please realize you can either have calm-alert or calm-sleepy as your desired state, depending on the circumstance. Below, an array of mental skills will be listed and described. I hope you will take the opportunity to try each one out. I will show you each skill discretely, in its simplest form. When you use these skills, feel free to embellish the experience by adding together various skills. All of the skills below can become part of your tool box of mental skills for helping you manage your life experiences. **Prior to starting your experiential practice, it is often helpful to rate your relaxation level on a 10 point scale (where 10 is most relaxed), so that you can then re-rate your relaxation (or whatever mental state) level after you have practiced a particular skill.**

List of Mental Skills for Relaxation

A) Kinesthetic Skills:

1. The Letting Go Response—Muscle Relaxation is actually based on body awareness and skill. When stressed or anxious, we tend to tighten our muscles in some way. How aware of your tension are you, and how able are you to let go of your tension? Try this out: Raise your arm out in front of you, and tighten it. Now, can you allow yourself to let go of your tricep muscle, allowing gravity to take place so that your arm just plops down to your lap? Here, we don't want to just place the arm down, or throw it down. If you have trouble going from tension to relaxation, please don't feel disheartened. Rather, you can realize that this takes practice, and with practice you can learn how to let go of muscle tension when it arises. Now, perhaps you can recall where and how you typically hold your tension. Tighten like you typically do. Then, let it go. Practice will help your awareness and your skill level, so that whenever you get nervous, you will have the skills to let go of the tension.

2. Whole Body Muscle Relaxation Practice—Some people teach this from toe to head, but I prefer head to toe. We can focus on your awareness of your muscle tension and relaxation contrast first, and then go back over the body parts, simply relaxing each part. If you have an injury or body weakness, and prefer not to tense your body parts, just proceed directly to focus on relaxing the body part. So, to begin with, you can tighten your head and scalp. Hold it 5 seconds. Now, let it go, relaxing your head and scalp. Next, you can harden your eyes. With your eyes open or closed, harden your eyes. Hold it a few seconds. Now, soften your eyes. As we proceed down your face, you can scrunch up your cheeks. Now, let it go. Then purse or tighten your lips and jaw (unless you have TMJ—in which case I would suggest you not do the tightening first). Hold it a few seconds, and then let that go, allowing your jaw to relax and loosen. Now moving to your neck and shoulders, tighten, hold it, and then relax. Let go of any neck and shoulder tightening. Next, moving on down to your upper chest and back, tighten there…hold it for a few seconds…then, let that go. Now, harden your stomach and lower back. Hold that for a few seconds, and then soften your belly and relax your lower back. We can complete the upper body by raising and tightening both arms, holding it for a few seconds, and then let go, releasing the tension down your arms to the tips of your fingers. We now travel to the hips and buttocks, where you tighten for a few seconds. When you let go of tension now, see if you can allow yourself to be fully supported by the chair or couch you are sitting on, rather than feeling like you have to hold yourself up. You can now tighten your upper legs, hold it for a few seconds, and then let go. Now, tighten your lower legs, hold it a few seconds, and then let go of any lower leg tension. We can complete the head to toe muscle relaxation process by focusing on your feet and toes: tighten, hold it for a few seconds, and now let that go. Ok, now, instead of tightening and then relaxing all the body parts, let's go back over the parts, this time just relaxing the parts. We had first tensed the parts so you could experience the contrast with relaxation. Now that you are aware of the experience of relaxing the parts, let's go to that directly:

- Relax the scalp and forehead
- Soften the eyes
- Relax the cheeks
- Let go of any mouth and jaw tension
- Relax the neck and shoulders
- Let go of any upper chest and upper back tension
- Soften the belly and relax the lower back
- Feel the calmness travel down your arms, to the tips of your fingers
- Relax the hips and buttock, so that you allow your chair or couch to support you. Feel your center of gravity lower.
- Relax your upper legs
- Relax your lower legs
- Feel the calmness travel all the way down to your feet and toes

You can now spend a few moments enjoying your fully body relaxation experience…After you have done that, you can re-rate your relaxation on a 10 point scale, where 10 is most relaxed.

Have you noticed any change? Most people do report some increased relaxation, which is an important indicator to you of the possibility of transforming your internal state. It can, indeed, be extraordinary to realize that we are not stuck with whatever mental state we happen to be in. Rather, it is possible to learn mental skills like this that allow us to move toward our desired state. This exercise can take a little while, but can help you powerfully access inner calm. Once you learn what it is like to relax your muscles, it is also possible to do it quicker during play. You can focus on relaxing head to toe, in a moment, like a letting go response.

3. Belly Breathing—Please place one hand on your belly and one hand on your chest. Breathe normally. Which hand is moving out more on your inhale? If it is your chest hand that is moving out more, then you are doing chest breathing, and you are not maximizing your capacity for experiencing inner calm. When we are afraid, we tend to do quick chest breaths, but we are not at that point providing ourselves with maximum self support. Belly breathing takes place when our belly pushes out on the inhale. When we do belly breathing, our diaphragm can drop down during the inhale, allowing our lungs to expand more efficiently. When we lie down, we tend to naturally do belly breathing. If you are having trouble coordinating doing belly breathing while sitting or standing, you can lie down to discover how to do belly breathing. Then memorize what it feels like to do belly breathing and generalize it to sitting and standing positions. We are all going to be breathing anyway, so you might as well learn to breathe therapeutically. Now, using the skill of belly breathing, let's learn and practice some additional breathing skills.

4. Belly Breathing to a Count of 5—Doing belly breathing, count to 5 on the inhale, 5 on the exhale, and then pause between breaths. (I like the idea of pausing between breaths, because that really helps you to slow down your tempo.). In order to do this skill, you need to take in air more slowly than usual, and let out air more slowly than usual. If you are having difficulty counting to a count of 5, with each count about the length of a heartbeat, feel free to start with a count of 3, and then see if you can go to 4, 5, and even 6, 7 or 8. (A variation of this skill is to count to 5 on the inhale and 10 on the exhale. That accentuates the exhale, where letting go occurs, but you don't have the pause between breaths. See which you prefer.)

5. Calm on the Exhale—Focusing on the exhale as the time letting go occurs, say the word "calm" (or some other word if you prefer) on the exhale, feeling a wave of calm go through your body head to toe as you say it.

6. Energizing Breathing—Focusing on being relaxed and alert, rather than relaxed and sleepy, breathe in positive energy on the inhale, and breathe out excess tension on the exhale. We are going to do breathing while playing tennis, so why not do it therapeutically. We see from the above that doing breathing, we can settle ourselves down, quieting our mind, with inner calm, or energize ourselves, depending how we focus.

7. Body Scan I—On the inhale, scan your whole body, searching for points of tension; on the exhale, breathe out through any points of tension, thereby warming and relaxing those spots. (The Body Scan I skill enables you to highlight specific points of tension, rather than just focus on whole body relaxation. Each of us tends to hold our tension in our own idiosyncratic way. Some of us hold our tension in our back, others in our neck or shoulders, or arms, etc. With this skill you get to let go of tension in a specific area of tension for you. You can either focus on an area that is currently tense as you scan your body, or you can highlight your personally identified area of tension, to give it some extra focus for relaxation.)

8. Body Scan II—This is an inverse of Body Scan I. On the inhale, search for a body part that feels ok; on the exhale, spread the good feeling throughout your body.

B) Visual Skills:

1. Basic imagery skills—Before we practice specific imagery skills conducive to the relaxation response, it is helpful to learn the basic components of using imagery. In order to do imagery effectively, it is important to have *control* over the content of the image, while also being able to image *vividly*. I once worked with a woman tennis player, who was about to play a tennis rival. I asked her to imagine playing a point exactly the way she would like to. Her eyes moved back and forth for 5 seconds, and then she gave a disappointed look. I asked her what happened, and she replied that she had lost the point. I reminded her she could play the point any way she wanted, with the task to play it ideally for her. By the third try, she started to be able to picture in a way conducive to her playing this opponent effectively. Another distinction is between associated and dissociated imagery. With *associated* imagery, you see from your own eyes, while with *dissociated* imagery you see yourself in a situation. Additionally, *submodality* distinctions can be important to using your imagery capabilities. If the visual sense is considered a modality, then submodalities include various ingredients of that sense. So, images can be color or black and white; still snapshots or movement; small or large; close or far; etc. Being able to maneuver with these submodalities can help you generate the effect you want with the image. I once had the task of contacting a person I didn't know. I was a little intimidated about it. As I examined how I was picturing contacting the person, I realized I was seeing the person in my mind in a black and white still image photograph, with a rather unaccepting, sour response to my approach. When I changed the image to color and movement, with the person welcoming my approach, it became easy to contact him. Sometimes, maneuvering the size or distance of the image can also make the difference that makes the difference in your experience. I worked with a female fencer who found she could mentally rehearse for an event more quickly if she could see herself perform from a closer distance.

2. Remembered Imagery—Remembering a pleasant scene—Find a pleasant, enjoyable scene you have experienced, whether recently or awhile ago. Go to that place and time, vividly being there just the way you like. See, hear and feel what it is like to be here in this scene. When you have the positive feeling from this scene, if you'd like, you can bring that feeling back with you to the present.

3. Created Imagery—Making up a pleasant scene—Rather than draw on the resource of a previous experience, you can make up a scene. You can make up a realistic scene, such as imagining a pleasant beach scene in Hawaii, or you can imagine something experientially relaxing, but less plausible, such as resting on a cloud, or flying around the rings of Saturn. Once you locate the scene, go to the scene and enjoyably play it out. See, hear and feel what it is like to be in the scene. When you have the pleasant, relaxed feeling, you can bring it to the present.

4. Relaxing Color—What color is relaxation? See that color in your mind's eye as a way of tuning into a state of relaxation.

5. Protective devices—Presented now are a few examples of creative imagery that can help protect you from incoming stress. In order to handle life stresses well, it is often helpful to draw on positive, imagined protective devices:

A. **Protective Aura—Color Coded Room**—What color is relaxation? See that color, feeling the relaxation that accompanies that. Then imagine you are in a room filled with this color. It is a magical room in that when you breathe in this room you breathe in the relaxation of the color. Breathing in this color, a protective aura of this color forms around you. Then imagine leaving this room, with the protective aura still surrounding you. Imagine going through your day with this protective aura cushioning you against any life stresses. It cushions you just like a trampoline would cushion your impact landing if you jumped on it.

B. **Plexiglass Shield**—Imagine a Plexiglass shield you erect at arm's length around you. This can shield you from incoming stress. Imagine an event where something stressful, toxic, or noxious is coming at you. Rather than let the stressor go through you and knock you over, imagine the stressor is stopped by your Plexiglass shield. You can allow whatever information is useful to go through the shield, so that you have full access to information, but you don't need to let anything toxic inside.

C. **Force Field**—Imagine you have a remote control button which you can press to set up a protective force field around you. Just like with the Star Trek ship, you can put up this force field when you sense danger or are under siege. You don't need to have the force field up all the time, because that could "drain the ship's energy." Imagine a situation where you can protect yourself using this force field protective device.

D. **Safety Bubble**—If you like, you can erect a safe space around you, so that you feel protected and safe, and able to focus on whatever is of importance to you. I have worked with numerous musicians who have found it helpful to put this safety bubble around them, thereby making it easier for them to tune into and express their music, not feeling inundated by the glares of the audience, or encumbered by the positioning of nearby musicians.

E. **Safe Space**—Instead of a safety bubble around you right here, it would be possible for you to locate some space you can go to in your mind where you feel safe. People working with traumas or phobias often find it extremely helpful, as part of their positive self care, to be able to go to their safe space if they start to feel too overwhelmed.

F. **Step Back Technique**—While the other protective devices are rather elective, each person finding whichever ones appeal to them, I believe this skill is most essential, important for everyone to learn. When in a situation that is stressful or unsettling, you can step back outside of yourself to gain greater perspective. Imagine an event where you sense all is not going well for you. Step back outside of yourself, so that you can see yourself in the situation. You might imagine stepping back several feet. (Alternatively, you could imagine floating back and up so that you see yourself from that perspective. Another way to do this, by the way, is to stay where you are, but imagine yourself in front of you relating with the situation. That, instead of a Step Back, would actually be an imagined Self Forward Technique. In the Self Forward Technique, you keep yourself where you are, but imagine yourself in the situation in front of you. Where you are now, seeing yourself in front of you, becomes the step back position.) When you step back, you leave the unsettling or stressful feeling where you were before, so that you feel neutral and curious in the step back perceptual position. While in the step back position, figure out what resource(s) is needed to handle the event optimally. Imagine applying that resource. If that seems like the appropriate resource, you are ready to step back in and handle the situation. If you need other resources, add those, check that they seem appropriate, and then step back into the situation. This whole process of stepping back and finding and adding appropriate resources, is called the New Behavior Generator Strategy in NLP.

6. Hypnotic Fix—So far, our visual resources have tended to rely on going inside to do imagery. Here, we will shift to focusing outside of yourself. Fix your gaze on a spot you feel ok about staring at… You can be curious about what will happen to your perceptions and experience as you do this. Is the object getting more diffuse? Are you getting more connected to the spot? Do you feel more at one with the spot? If you continue with this for a couple of minutes, you may find that this helps calm you down, and you might find that this helps with your focusing on a task. I worked with a gymnast who found that staring at his apparatus helped to drop out his bothersome internal dialogue, and helped him focus on the event. Billie Jean King, the Hall of Fame woman's tennis player, used to focus on a tennis ball prior to matches, as a way of connecting to the ball, helping make the ball feel like part of her. I have found athletes and musicians often find it very helpful to focus on their instrument, their music, or some element of their sport, such as a basketball player staring at the rim. Doing the hypnotic fix can help with focusing, as well as relaxing. I think of it as priming the focusing mechanism. I worked with a pistol team shooter once. In the office, I suggested he stare at the door knob as a way of connecting to it. He then left the office, went to the shooting range, and called me excitedly to report he had just shot considerably higher than ever before. I have found that once you do this focusing work earlier in the day, it does not take as long to get connected when you do it later in the day. You can use this also as a way of connecting to something important. If you have been procrastinating, you can stare at your work, or tasks. The structure of procrastinating seems to involve placing things outside your range of vision, so putting things in front of you seems like a useful counter to procrastination.

7. Mental Rehearsal—This utilizes our capacity to mentally review and ready ourselves for upcoming events. I recommend we take time right before an event, and also days before an event, to do mental rehearsal. A week before a tennis event, I might take 30 seconds to a minute a few times a day to mentally prepare to play the way I want to. Doing that seems to help my inner self be more ready to play that way. If I want to serve and volley, it helps me be ready to do it naturally if I have prepared to do it ahead of time. Here, I will now present two kinds of mental rehearsal.:

A) **Mastery Rehearsal**—Select an event you want to mentally rehearse. Now imagine it going just the way you want, with you being in your best mental state and using your skills and strategy well. This is your "just right" state, with you being "on" your game.

B) **Coping Rehearsal**—Now let's review the same event again. This time, imagine the various obstacles that can occur. They can be obstacles in the environment, have to do with things others do, or involve some disruption in your own mental state, strategy, relating abilities, physical state or performance skills. Imagine overcoming these obstacles well, so you are not thrown off center by them. You are able to maintain your positive mental state, despite any adversity. I worked with a doctoral student who was needing to re-take his comprehensive exams. Failing again would mean dismissal from the program, and he especially feared the oral exam. He was confident he would be fine on the written portion. We identified the mental state that would be optimal for the oral exam, and he mentally rehearsed maintaining his positive mental state with things both going smoothly (mastery rehearsal), or if running into different possible obstacles (coping rehearsal). The mental state involved being engaging, open to learning, reflective, curious, self accepting about things he didn't know, creative, and open to sharing his process. I suggested he mentally rehearse his mental state for one minute 5 times per day in the week before the exam. He was thrilled that he did great on the exam, and reported that the mental skills tips were incredibly helpful.

C) Auditory Skills:

1. Positive Inner Voice—How you speak with yourself is important to being able to support and guide yourself effectively. This includes both the content of what you say to yourself and your manner. Content wise, it is helpful to say things that support ourselves, inspire ourselves and guide ourselves. Using our NLP Outcome Frame Model, we can say things to ourselves that elucidate where we are, where we would like to be, and how we can get there. We don't want to spend our time criticizing, blaming or lamenting our plight. How we express our positive content is also important. You can practice adopting a voice with a positive tone, tempo and timbre. Suggesting to yourself to calm down while in a frantic, anxious voice will not have the desired effect. It will be easier to stay in a positive mental state if your self talk is positive in content and manner.

2. Soothing Voice of an Other—Conjure up the soothing voice of an other. This can be the voice of a family member or friend, or a voice of a fictional character or someone else you have heard. Listen to this voice say ego supportive things to you—e.g. "I am on your side". "I believe in you". "I like the way you're doing this", etc.. While listening to these encouraging, supportive messages, your task is to allow yourself to fully receive the messages. When I was going through NLP training in the early 1980's, Leslie Cameron Bandler shared an idea of having people imagine looking through the eyes of someone who loves you. Doing that can be a supportive, validating, fostering experience. In the Soothing Voice of an Other, we are able to take in the caring, compassionate support of an other.

3. Soothing Voice of Yourself—As part of your Self Coaching, it is important to be able to soothe yourself. This is akin to the Positive Inner Voice skill described above, but here we are specifically referring to soothing yourself. Adjust your own voice tone, tempo an timbre so that you can relate to yourself in a soothing way. Then adding voice content that is ego supportive, such as "I believe in you", and "I am on your side", your task is to allow yourself to really receive the messages. Take in the messages, and let them wash over you in a supportive way. The ability to work with how you speak with yourself, with compassionate content, and receive the messages, is a vital part of effective self management.

4. Mental State Accessing through Music—Select some relaxing music you can listen to in your imagination. Let's see how relaxed you get from listening to the this music....Now, let's shift to inspiring music. As you change the music, let's see how your mental state shifts.

5. Autogenic Phrases—This skill uses the power of repeated self statements to adjust your mental state. Here we will be using a series of repeated self statements to help you reach a relaxed state. Repeat each statement several times before moving on to the next statement. Let's begin by having you imagine warm shower water on your hands as you say, "my hands are getting warmer and warmer." After repeating this 3-4 times, you can imagine your arms are holding up some books, as you say, "and my arms are getting heavier and heavier." If you want, at this point, instead of heavy arms you can go for light arms, by having you "imagine your fingers tied to helium balloons", as you say, "my arms are getting lighter and lighter." After repeating that, you can imagine placing a cool compress on your forehead as you say, "my forehead is cool and comfortable." And you repeat that. After repeating that, you can say, "and my heart rate is slowing down". After repeating that, you can say, "whole body and mind, calm and comfortable." The power of repeated self statements can be used to help you access various mental states. If you wanted to feel confident, for example, you might imagine, "my shoulders are broad and strong." If you wanted to increase your concentration, you might repeat, "and my eyes are energized and focused."

D) Combining and Sequencing Mental Skills

Learning and practicing the individual mental skills, we can focus on the potential benefits of putting the skills together. Combining skills occurs when we do one skill and then add another while still doing the first skill. We can combine as many skills as we choose—2,3,4, etc.. For example, we could combine relaxing our muscles with a calming breath. Or we could combine remembering a relaxing scene with hearing some pleasant or inspiring music. Sequencing skills refers to doing one skill and then stopping that when you add another skill. The order you apply your mental skills may make a difference for you. Some people find that they can image better after doing some muscle relaxation or belly breathing, while others find they can relax their muscles better if they first do some imagery. Just to give you an idea of how these combinations or sequences work for you, how about trying out a few examples:

I. 1) Whole Body Muscle Relaxation; 2) Visual Remembered Pleasant Scene; 3) Soothing Voice of Self

II. 1) Hypnotic Fix; 2) Calm on the Exhale; 3) Relaxing Music

III. 1) Create a Relaxing Scene; 2) Belly Breathing to a Count of 5; 3) Mental Rehearsal of upcoming event.

Do you find that you prefer one sequence or combination to another? I hope you will experiment with various possibilities of using more than one mental skill at a time.

E) When and How to Use Mental Skills

The answer is all the time, and mindfully. We are going to breathe, talk to ourselves, and image things, so we might as well do them therapeutically. Before I hit a serve, I can picture my serve landing in the box and bouncing and moving in a certain way. That image leads to the feeling in my body of hitting the serve in a way that makes that serve happen. If instead I pictured being tight and hitting a weak serve, that wouldn't go as well. If I miss a shot, compassionately say "that's ok" to myself, and image fixing it, that is helpful. If instead I miss a shot and just criticize myself harshly, that does not help me fix it. I need to realize how, through my mental skills, I can help myself get the outcomes I want. We make choices. I can choose which Relaxation skill calms me in the moment. I can choose to step back and get perspective when things on the court are not going my way. I can keep eagerness in my voice even if I am down a break. I can put up a plexiglass shield if my opponent is taunting me. My tone of voice can be important as I select a Self Coaching Perspective like the Curiosity Frame. We use our Mental Skills to prepare for a match, to make adjustments in a match, and to positively review a match. Our Mental Skills are the sensory resources that help us work with our Self Coaching Perspectives and Tennis Performance Categories. Thinking of our NLP Outcome Frame, does what you say, think, picture, and do help move you from your Present State to your Desired State? These are skills, so keep practicing the positive use of your Mental Skills.

CHAPTER 6

Mental State Training

I am excited to work with you on you learning to manage your Mental States (MS). A MS is a mind-body-feeling-behavior experience we have in the moment. How we feel inside, our mind- body state, is vital to our performance experience and effectiveness. We support, energize, and direct our performances through our self coaching via our MS. While it is possible to perform ok even when our MS is not optimal, it certainly is easier and more natural to perform when in our best MS. Remember Michael Jordan's shrugging to the broadcasters on court after he hit six 3 point shots and scored 35 points in the first half of a finals playoff game vs Portland in 1992? His shrug was saying he was on automatic, and from within his great MS it was easy to score. Csiksentmihalyi spoke of the flow state in his book, *Flow: The Psychology of Optimal Experience.* He said that in a flow state you are focused, enjoying, confident, motivated and feeling up to facing the challenge. He described the flow state as an autotelic state, meaning one does the experience for its own sake, not just for the sake of the outcome. (Recall the Self Coach Perspective I listed: "Focus on the process, don't worry about the outcome".) We have all found that when our MS is positive, we tend to feel well and perform well. When our MS is not so good, we don't tend to have a good experience and tend to underperform. In the 1993 Wimbledon final vs Steffi Graf, Jana Novotna, who was up 4-1 in the 3rd set, seemed to lose her MS and started missing shots uncharacteristically. She lost the last 5 games of the match and was understandably upset after. We assume her MS declined there. In the pressure of the moment it was difficult for her to play at her typical playing level.

Robert Dilts, an NLP pioneer, and Stephen Gilligan, developer of Generative Therapy, work together, and speak of the COACH vs CRASH states. The COACH state is a positive state, that includes being C (Centered—O (Open)—A (Attending with awareness)—C (Connected)—H (Holding -creating support). They believe it helpful to do therapeutic work by first helping a person step into their COACH state. By extension, it is useful to be in the COACH state doing any activity or performance. The CRASH state, by contrast, is a negative MS that interferes with optimal experience and performance. The CRASH state involves C (Contracted)—R (Reaction)—A (Analysis Paralysis)—S (Separation)—H ((Hurt and Hatred). In The CRASH state you have negative feelings, overthink and overreact, and are disconnected from inner resources. It is difficult to be at your best if in that negative MS. I once attended a hypnosis seminar led by Theodore Barber, He encouraged people to do everything with Self Hypnosis. He was thinking of Self Hypnosis as being in a state of inner comfort.

So, the premise here in our MS training is that we want to engage in our performances and experiences with a positive MS. What many people say, however, is that they can't control their MS. Your MS may seem elusive to you. One day you just find yourself in a good MS and are On your game, whereas, on another occasion you feel more Off. This MS Training, though, is designed to help you realize we can manage our MS. We have Perspectives and Skills we can use to access and adjust our MS. This understanding is huge! If you can build your Skills working with your MS, you can more consistently play with the Frame of Mind and MS that helps you have a good experience and positive performance. We can manage our experience so we can play at the level we are capable of. Sometimes, we can even get into a zone, where everything clicks, and we play uncannily. Those times of flow and peak performance become available to us when our combination of challenge and skills matches and our mental state is positive, with ingredients like Enjoyment, Concentration, Relaxation and Confidence. A big part of Self Coaching is learning to manage our MS.

In this training, I am going to help you understand your Mental States and help you learn to manage your MS. I want to teach you about Individual Core MS. We will then discuss how to Combine the MS. Understanding your Sequencing of MS may also be important for you. Then we will do the Difference Procedure, so you can understand how your MS operate when you are playing well and playing poorly. This will provide you with a MS Profile and help you understand how your MS work, and help you know which MS are performance keys for you. After that we will work on you learning to access and anchor your MS. Knowing how to do this helps you be in the MS you want more readily. You will also see how you can select and access your optimal mental state for any event. We will also focus on how you can monitor and make mental adjustments (MA) as needed. The mental state training we are doing here is designed to provide you with the tools to access, maintain and adjust your MS as needed during a match. After playing you can assess how your MS was by filling out the Mental State Playing Inventory. This includes identifying your Mental State Profile and also rating your playing level via the Mental State Playing Level Scale. We will also discuss the concept of accessing states that help you play up to par, and even better, accessing flow and peak experience/performance.

CORE INDIVIDUAL MENTAL STATES (MS)

Textbooks by sport psychologists tend to have chapters on concepts such as Relaxation, Confidence, Concentration and Motivation, as vital to our experience and performance. Here I am identifying a list of these, and calling them Mental States. They are mind-body states that have cognitive-emotional-physiological-behavioral correlates. Being in various levels of these MS affects how we feel, think and play. We can learn to help ourselves step into optimal levels of these MS. Each of these MS tend to have some importance to each of us, but we will have our own idiosyncratic way they operate within each of us. So one MS, like Confidence, may be especially key for one of us, while Relaxation may be more vital for another. We also may have some MS that we tend to access readily, while others may be ones we need to add to be at our best. We will speak to these issues when we talk about Combining and Sequencing our MS. For now, we will speak to a list of Core Mental States. I would like you to understand each MS, and how you can access them with your self coaching tools (skills and perspectives). When we later do the Difference Procedure you will hopefully get to understand how these MS operate within you. By the way, feel free to add to the list of Core MS if you have some other MS that are helpful to you.

Here is a list of Core Mental States:

1. **Relaxation:** I am comfortable and freed up
2. **Concentration:** I am present and focused
3. **Confidence:** I can
4. **Motivation:** I want
5. **Determination:** I will
6. **Enjoyment:** I like
7. **Patience:** I have time; feel unrushed
8. **Imperturbable:** I am unbothered

1. **Relaxation:** Relaxation is the sense of "I am calm in space". When optimally Relaxed, your muscles are relaxed, not too tense. Think of worry, anxiety and tension as internal noise that makes it difficult to be present and focus on what you need.

Worry reflects concerns we have about the possible negative future and results. We do better, however, when we are present in the moment. We could view worry as information that we have a concern. That message is like getting a phone call with the information. Our task is to get the message and problem solve in the moment, rather than continue to worry. If we continue to worry anxiously, that is like letting the phone continue to ring. That is internal noise. Rather than worry, with Relaxation your thoughts are clear and focused positively and naturally. You experience inner quiet. When Relaxed your strokes are natural and free, not constrained by tension. In this MS your mind is free to focus on whatever you choose, whether selecting a shot or game plan, or problem solving something else. In the Mental Skills Training chapter I have identified myriad ways we can step into Relaxation. We can do muscle relaxation, belly breathing, remembered imagery of times you were relaxed, or created imagery of scenes that relax you, for example. Please refer to that chapter for an extensive training on using mental skills for Relaxation. Each of us has experienced the benefit of being calm and composed when playing, and the curse of being too tight or worried to hit a ball well. There are a number of Self Coaching Perspectives that are also helpful to accessing and maintaining a Relaxed MS. For example, the Learning Frame puts us in a frame of mind where it is ok to give oneself time to develop, being self accepting, and allowing mistakes as part of the learning process. We are then free to relax. Focusing on the Process, Not Worrying About the Outcome is a very helpful perspective that enables you to let go of concerns about missing shots. I saw Martina Navratilova play a match once when she was playing tight, and the match was close. Then I saw her go for a backhand freely. She missed the shot, but I told the person I was with that she was ok now. Even though she had missed that shot, she had gotten herself into a freed up mode. Not being afraid to miss, she was freed up to play. She won handily after that. Combining our Mental Skills with positive Self Coaching Perspectives can help us maintain our positive MS. The Mental Skills can help us step into a positive MS, but if our perspective is negative, that can take us away from our positive MS. We can use our Mental Skills for Relaxation and Self Coaching Perspectives to access Relaxation to start the match, and to make adjustments as needed during the match. During a match, for example, you can take a calming breath, relax your muscles and picture yourself hitting freely between points. You can also remind yourself to Focus on the Process and not Worry about the Outcome.

2. **Concentration:** Concentration is the sense of "I am present and focused". I think of Concentration as having two main factors. There is a saturation factor, like concentrated orange juice. Here you are immersed and fully present. This presence helps you to be in the moment, seeing clearly and hitting the ball cleanly, while reacting well to whatever is occurring. The second factor is focusing, which involves selecting a focus and engaging in task relevant focusing. If I select the focus of playing from within an optimal MS, then I can't let things distract me from my selected focus. Do you know the game, "Simon Says"? Here we are given instructions to do things, like "lift your left arm", but we don't do them unless Simon says to do it. Theoretically, it should be an easy game to win. We just need to maintain our focus. Similarly, if our focus is on our mental state, ball striking and game plan, to win the Simon Says game of tennis, we need to maintain our focus and not be distracted by things that are not task relevant. We can't let missing a shot, getting a bad call,

being down in a match, a string breaking, or getting tired, take us away from our focus. There is mental toughness in being able to do this. Understanding what to focus on is important. The sport psychologist, Robert Nideffer, has had some great things to say about this in his Attention Control Training. One thing he wrote about is how we can have Broad, Narrow, Internal, and External focus. So when a basketball point guard dribbles down the court he has a Broad-External focus, to see where his teammates are. If he elects to shoot, he needs to shift to a Narrow-External focus. This will help him connect to the basket and shoot better. In tennis, if playing doubles we need to be able to see where our opponents are situated and leaning (Broad-External), yet switch to a Narrow-External focus as we follow the path of the ball to track it to hit it. We then need a Broad-Internal focus as we think about the game plan that will work in this situation, and a Narrow-Internal focus as we monitor our MS and reactions. Learning to be in charge of selecting our focusing, while being fully present, is helpful to our tennis. Just like learning Relaxation is a skill, and we know when we are relaxed by our muscles being loose, swinging freely, while feeling inner calm, so is Concentration a skill that can be cultivated. I know I am Concentrating well when my legs are bent nicely, and my eyes are alert and nicely tracking the ball and what is going on. I can step into Concentration by adopting this stance. I can also picture being alert and focused and access Concentration that way. Most of the Self Coaching Perspectives can be good ideas worthy of selecting as a focus for playing. "Focus on Your Process, Don't Worry About the Outcome, is very helpful to being in the moment with your strokes. Selecting the "Healthy Frame" would help you be the person you want to be handling the match or practice. Those are just two examples. You select your focus and have a process goal of maintaining that through your event.

3. **Confidence:** Confidence is the sense of "I can". Confidence has to do with trust in one's ability to do something. When Confident, you have a sense in your mind and body that you can do something. We don't need to think of having a general sense of Confidence, but rather as something specific. For example, we can think of Confidence in terms of your feeling you can hit your next forehand, or your next serve. Your Confidence could be low in your backhand volley because you don't really know how to hit it. That is a need for stroke development issue. You can figure out how to work around that in the meantime, while coming up with an improvement plan. Alternatively, your Confidence could be lower in a stroke because you have somehow lost connection to the stroke. This could involve some stroke technique issue as well as a mental state issue of lost connection to the stroke. Imaging with Repetition of the stroke often works well to help you regain your connection and feel for the stroke. If you image hitting your crosscourt backhand a number of times in a row, seeing the ball, and feeling yourself hitting it, at a certain point you are apt to notice you feel connected to the stroke, and have a higher rating of your Confidence in the stroke. You may go from a 4 to an 8, for example, on a 10 point scale. You can also think of the stroke technique you would like to adjust and practice that. Your task, then, is to Do What You Know. You are doing things to connect to what you know. That is doable. If we have lost connection in our strokes, our task is to use our Mental Skills and Perspectives to see if we can regain that connection. If you don't believe in yourself in general, perhaps having low esteem, that is a bigger psychological issue that may require counseling. Still, the Self Coach Perspective

of practicing being Self Accepting, and allowing yourself to be in the Learning Frame, may allow you to be less self critical. If your general sense of confidence is low, it can still be useful to reframe Confidence to refer to a mental state about something specific. So while I may not believe in myself in general, I can have Confidence I can hit a forehand, run to a ball, or select a game plan that works for me. If you are not Confident you can beat an opponent because you see what a good player she or he is, you can evoke the idea of Possibility vs Probability. You may see a way to hold serve, by serving and volleying, or hitting high balls to their backhand, and if you do that there is a Possibility of being effective. This sense of Possibility may help increase your Confidence about how to play in this match. If I have enough successes with being Confident in specific tasks, perhaps this will help my belief in myself, but working on this in counseling may be important. I want to add here that Confidence as a MS can be an approach to a situation. When I am Confident as an approach, I am apt to be bold, strong and decisive. If I am not confident in how to get to the airport in a city, I can confidently, rather than meekly ask for directions. In tennis, if I am not feeling my forehand now, if I hit the forehand Confidently, "As If" I am confident, hitting boldly and decisively, maybe that will help me regain the stroke. When lacking in confidence you are apt to be too timid, weak and indecisive in your play.

4. **Motivation:** Motivation is the sense of "I want". Motivation involves connection to goals. When motivated you are connected to your goals. When unmotivated you have lost connection to your goals. I remember doing sport psychology work with a collegiate swimmer who was tired from working out twice a day, and came to me considering quitting the team. He was certainly allowed to do that, but changed his mind when I asked

him what his goals had been for the year. When he reminded himself about his goals for the conference championships at the end of the year, he regained his motivation to continue. It also helped to talk with his coach about tailoring his training to some things that he felt could be relevant to his improvement. In tennis, we can have outcome goals of achieving certain victories, championships, and rankings. For 30 years I woke up daily at 5:30am to play tennis before work. I didn't miss days because I remained connected to my goals of doing well in my senior tennis championships and getting good rankings. We also have process goals of improving in each of the Performance Categories (strokes, mental states, physical states, relationship management, and game plan). Motivation also involves the energy to mobilize ourselves to move towards our goals. The experience of being Motivated is a feeling of energy and activation that helps us mobilize ourselves. This mobilization helps us accomplish our goals. When Motivated we can persist with sustained effort and not quit due to obstacles or difficulties.

5. **Determination:** Determination is the sense of "I will." If Motivation is "I want", Determination is "I will". To me, this is the next step of intensity that is vital to some people. For some people, if they want something, they also automatically feel determined. For them Motivation and Determination might be the same. Other people might be more low key naturally, and for them, wanting something doesn't necessarily lead to the extra step of mobilization that could help them move best toward their goals. The state of Determination is apt to include a set jaw, and extra sense of resolve. For me, accessing Determination is extra important to me playing at my best. When in my 30's I played an open tournament. Playing a seeded younger player, I was losing, but enjoying the match. On a changeover, I said

to my opponent I needed to take a sip of water. He angrily said I had 30 seconds. I thought he was being rude, and accessed a greater level of Determination than I had had. I changed my game plan, and started to play more junk tennis, hitting drop shots, lobs, and generally jerking him around. He got frustrated and broke a racket. I won the match. My Determination won me the match. I probably should have accessed that MS to begin with, but thankfully used my response to his rudeness effectively. Are you a player who gets helped by being Determined, or are you someone who, if Motivated are naturally Determined?

6. **Enjoyment:** Enjoyment is the sense of "I like". Enjoyment includes the lightness and playfulness that is very important to some players who like participating in their tennis. It is important for many people to remember that they participate in tennis because they love tennis. For some players this sets the frame for their participation. Stephen Gilligan speaks of 3 archetypal factors that help people function well: being playful, fierce and tender. The mind body state of a player can feel light and playful, but can also include being gritty and absorbed. Some people find that when they can experience Enjoyment, they can readily be playful, fierce and tender. Csiksentmihalyi, writing about Flow, emphasizes the importance of joy, facing challenge with positive skills and how flow occurs when the experience is autotelic, meaning done for its own sake. How are you Enjoying your tennis? For some hard working, hard driving people, Enjoyment may not be emphasized as essential. For others, it is most vital. Is Enjoyment important to you?

7. **Patience:** Patience is the sense of "I have time". Whereas Relaxation refers to inner calm and being able to move freely in space, Patience refers to the sense of not being rushed in time. So Relaxation and Patience go together on the space-time

continuum. We have all had times playing tennis where we felt rushed and that impacted our sense of tension when playing. When we are Patient we sense we have time to develop a point. We don't feel rushed and don't need to rush it. We can help our sense of Patience by doing the Mental Skill of Breathing to a Count of 5. Doing this can help slow your personal tempo. We can also mentally rehearse being in a Patient state. Being Self Accepting and in the Learning Frame are Self Coaching Perspectives that can help give us time to play freely.

8. **Imperturbable:** This is the sense of being unbothered. It can really help us to be in a MS where things don't bother us. When Imperturbable, things that occur just roll off our backs and don't distract us from our optimal MS. We are resilient when we are Imperturbable. We feel sturdy. When Larry Turville and I were playing in the semis of ITF Individual doubles World Championships in Antalya, Turkey in 2010, we were playing the top British team. They were excellent players and friends, but also fierce competitors. After the first set, Larry asked if the clay court could be swept to help with the bounces. The British team refused. Larry began to argue and plead his case, but sweeping the court at that time would require the agreement of all 4 players. I felt like they would disagree with any request we made, so, smiling, I said that to Larry, and we played on just fine. We won the match. I felt like not being thrown off was important there. When Imperturbable, you are not thrown off by missing shots, bad calls, being tired, losing, or noticing a decline in some MS like Motivation or Enjoyment. Instead, you are able to appreciate detecting whatever is going on so you can problem solve with your Self Coaching. The Mental Skills of using Protective Devices can help us remain unbothered. This includes Mental Skills such as placing a Protective Bubble or

Plexiglass Shield around you, having a Second Skin so things don't penetrate you negatively, or using the Step Back Technique so you have distance and perspective from events. You can refer to the Mental Skills Training chapter for more discussion of protective devices. Mentally rehearsing being Imperturbable can also be helpful. I am including Imperturbable as a Core MS because it seems so helpful in being able to maintain the other MS at an optimal level, helping you keep a clear head, and be free to play how you want. The Healthy Frame is an example of a Self Coaching Perspective that can help us not be bothered by things. When healthy, we are able to keep our healthy perspective about things and not let things get to us adversely.

9. **Other:** The above lists a number of Core MS I have identified, but does not need to be a complete list. Each player can have their own list of essential MS. Each player can have their own words that help generate their optimal MS. Some of these words seem fairly synonymous to words on our list already, while others make more of a new addition. So please feel free to add words like: Energetic, Happy, Playful, Fierce, Forceful, and Self Compassionate if these round out what comprises your best MS. Each of these words, and others, can be viewed as MS with a mind-feeling-body-behavior component. We can help ourselves access each using our Mental Skills and Self Coaching Perspectives, like we have done with the other Core MS.

COMBINING THE MENTAL STATES

We have been discussing the individual core MS and how each one is important to our experience and performance. We can learn to select, access and maintain each MS when that MS needs to be added. I believe, however, that our Optimal Mental State (OMS) is actually a combination of these states. We don't just play Relaxed. We don't just play Concentrating (focused). We don't just play Confident. Rather, we are a blend of these. We are, for example, Relaxed, Concentrating, and Confident. There is an experience we have when we have these combined. Each Mental State is embodied, so there are behavioral, postural, sensory, feeling and thinking referents. Let's do an exercise. Using your mental skill of belly breathing to a count of 5 or muscle relaxation or imaging yourself relaxed, enter a state of Relaxation. Take your time.......Once you have this, now imagine adding Concentration to that state of Relaxation. Can you feel the energy in your eyes more? Do you feel your legs more? What else? What do you add when you add Concentration? Take your time to experience this.....Now add Confidence. Imagine yourself bold, strong and decisive. How does your posture and inner strength feeling shift when you add Confidence?. Take your time to feel it. You now have a Relaxed-Concentration-Confident mental state. Is that a MS that would helpful to you? We can take any and all of our individual MS and put them together in a way that affects our experience and playing. We will show this more when we do the Difference Procedure, and when we work on selecting and accessing your Optimal Mental State.

SEQUENCING THE MENTAL STATES

It is possible to access your combined Optimal Mental State all at one time. You might mentally rehearse the full state and step into it all at once. Sometimes, though, you access one MS at a time, adding in ingredients one at a time. There it helps to understand how your mental states operate within you. Is it best for you to Relax first, which helps you Concentrate, which enables you to be Confident, which increases your Enjoyment, which makes it easy to stay Motivated? Or are you a person who needs to be Motivated first, having a strong sense of goals, which helps you Concentrate, which helps you be Confident, which allows you to Relax? Alternatively, do you need to be in a state of Enjoyment, which helps you be Motivated, which increases your Concentration? Or maybe you need to be Confident, connect to your Motivation, and then get to Determination in order to play your best. Each of us has our own sequence that seems to help us. Can you find a mental state that has a Domino Effect? That would be a MS you could have, which accessed, leads to optimal levels of other mental states. As long as you are Relaxed do you get good levels of the other mental states? Or is there a Key Ultimate State you need to get to to be at your best, like Enjoyment or Determination? Here you don't need to start with those states, but need to get to those states, in whatever sequence, in order to be at your best. A Key State for you can be either what you need to start with, or what state you need to ultimately get to. If we can think of ourselves as being our own Sherlock Holmes, we can be interested in understanding how our mental states operate. When we do the Difference Procedure we can assess how are mental states work for us. The Difference Procedure assesses our MS Profile when playing well vs when playing poorly.

THE DIFFERENCE PROCEDURE

1. Think of a time you performed/played well. Go to that time. See, hear, and feel yourself being in the event. Now rate each of the core Individual MS on a 10 point scale, during this event. Relaxation......Confidence.....Concentration......etc. The Core MS you are rating are: R (Relaxation), Cf (Confidence), CC (Concentration, M (Motivation), D (Determination), E (Enjoyment), P (Patience), I (Imperturbable)

2. Now think of a time you performed/played poorly, or more mediocre. Go to this performance. See, hear, and feel yourself in the event. Now rate each of the core Individual MS on a 10 Point scale when performing/playing poorly. Relaxation..... Confidence.....etc.

3. Compare the two performances and how your MS profile is different when doing well vs doing poorly. Notice what changes. Describe the differences. As you do this we can get some additional sense about how your mental states work. Is there a Mental State that seems most key for you? Is there a Mental State that serves as a domino, that leads to positive levels of other mental states? Do we have a sense of your sequence of mental states? When you are Relaxed, does that help you Concentrate? Or when you are Confident does that lead to you Enjoying?

Your Difference Procedure Profiles: Now please rate your Mental States on a 10 point scale, where 10 = best, for your best and worst performance examples. (If your mental state is too high you can add a +, to make it 10+, like if being overconfident is a problem.)

```
10
 9
 8
 7
 6
 5
 4
 3
 2
 1
     R   Cf   Cc   M   D   E   P   I   Other
                          Best—"On" Performance
```

10								
9								
8								
7								
6								
5								
4								
3								
2								
1								
	R	Cf	Cc	M	D	E	P	I	Other

Worst—"Off" Performance

(R = Relaxation; Cf = Confidence; Cc = Concentration; M = Motivation; D = Determination; E = Enjoyment; P = Patience; I = Imperturbable; Other = any other relevant states to you)

Mental State Profile Assessment

What are you noticing about your best and worst performances? What is the greatest difference between the 2 profiles? Do you have a sense of which mental states are key for you, and in what way? Which mental states are important for you to access first, and are especially important to access ultimately? What are you noticing about how your mental states work?

Difference Procedure—Examples—To help you understand the Difference Procedure more, let's take a look at a few examples.

(R=Relaxation; Cf = Confidence; CC = Concentration; M = Motivation; D = Determination; E = Enjoyment; P = Patience; I = Imperturbable; Other = any other relevant states to you)

Example 1:

```
10                              10
9       X       X                9
8   X       X       X  X         8                   X
7                   X X          7
6                                6
5                                5               X
4                                4                       X  X
3                                3   X               X       X
2                                2       X
1                                1
    R. Cf. Cc. M. D. E. P. I. Other   R. Cf. Cc. M. D. E. P. I. Other
```

"ON" - Best Performance Example   "OFF" - Worst Performance Example

Mental State Profile assessment: What do we notice here? All the player's mental states were pretty high on the best example and lower on the worst example. Confidence and Motivation were the highest rated MS for the "ON" example. When "Off" Confidence dipped the most. This player stays Motivated and had some Concentration in either case but wasn't as Determined when playing poorly and was bothered by things more when Off. It seems like Confidence is an important MS for this player. When asked about this, the player agreed that when their timing was good, they felt very comfortable and it was easy to play. Connecting to their strokes seems important, and imaging with repetition can help with this. Also, it may be that doing things that create inner comfort, like Relaxation skills, could help them stay connected to their game. Also of note is that the level of Determination lowering as much as it did in the Off time, suggests some lessening of resolve when things weren't going well. This seemed to go along with being bothered by things, as indicated by the lowered Imperturbability. Perhaps accessing certain Self Coaching Perspectives, like the Learning Frame and Healthy Frame, and using the Protective Devices, like the plexiglass shield or step back technique, could help the player not be bothered by what was happening, which might give more chance to find their game.

Difference Procedure—Example 2

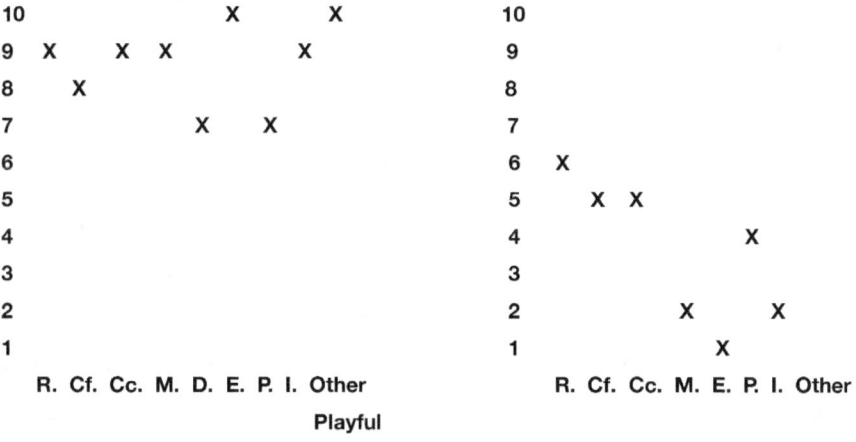

"ON: Best Performance example   "Off: Worst Performance example

Mental State Profile assessment: Notice that Enjoyment and being Playful are the highest scores in the "ON" example, and Enjoyment is the lowest score in the "Off" example. This player is emphasizing that having a good time and good experience is what is most important to them. When having a good time, this player is not bothered by things (see Imperturbability score), and this player can then stay Motivated. It might help this player to keep reminders of their goals so as to stay connected to what is important to them and not be bothered by what is happening on the court. Rather than be reactive to the playing environment, this player could take charge of being playful and joyous regardless of what else is occurring. This player could mentally rehearse being their playful self. I am reminded of a dream I had before the

World Team Championships in Antalya, Turkey, in 2010, in which the song "When You're Smiling" came to mind. Upon awakening I realized my unconscious mind was telling me it was important to keep a smiling attitude, and not let things bother me during the event. I was the captain of the U.S. 4 player team (Larry Turville, Brian Cheney, and Padge Bolton were the other team members). I was still playing ok, but was having some hip problems that required some attending to, and indeed got a hip replacement 6 months later. The "When You're Smiling" song was helpful to have me not be bothered by things throughout the event, like my hip or anything else. Indeed, in the finals of the event, there was some delay with rain, it got a bit dark outside due to the delay, and we got down in the middle of the 3rd set, against an excellent team from Spain. Nevertheless, Larry Turville and I came from behind to win a 3rd set tiebreaker, to win the ITF World Team Championship for the U.S.. I believe that staying in a Good Mood was a Self Coaching Perspective that proved very helpful there. The player with this Mental State Profile could get benefit from having a Staying in a Good Mood Perspective.

Difference Procedure—Example 3

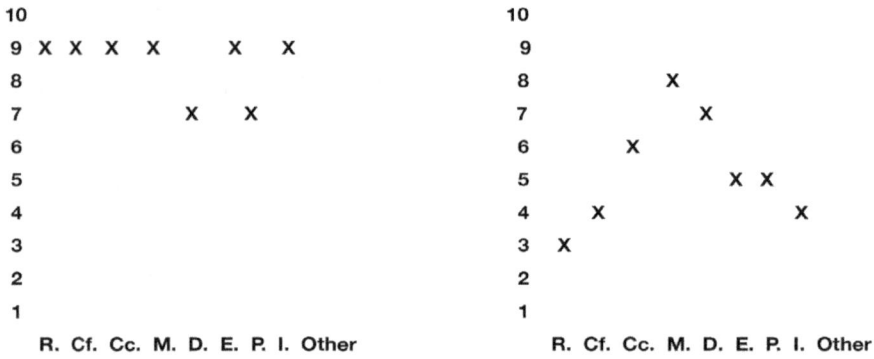

10								
9	X	X	X	X		X	X	
8								
7				X	X			
6								
5								
4								
3								
2								
1								
	R.	Cf.	Cc.	M.	D.	E.	P.	I. Other

"ON" - Best Performance example

10								
9								
8				X				
7					X			
6		X						
5						X	X	
4	X							X
3	X							
2								
1								
	R.	Cf.	Cc.	M.	D.	E.	P.	I. Other

"OFF" - Worst Performance example

Mental State Profile Assessment: This player stays Motivated, whether playing well or poorly, but the Relaxation and Confidence really fall off when playing poorly. It seems important for this person to have Self Coaching Perspectives that help take the pressure off and keep them freed up: the Learning Frame, Challenge Frame vs Threat Frame, and Focusing on the Process, Not Worrying About the Outcome, are examples of useful Perspectives. Mental Skills for Relaxation (belly breathing, muscle relaxation, imaging being comfortable playing, etc) and Confidence (imaging strokes with repetition; picturing self playing with confidence) are possibilities. This player seems to try hard, whether playing well or poorly. Being Self Accepting and committing to being more unbothered (Imperturbable), could be helpful. This could involve embracing the Healthy Frame perspective.

I hope that providing you with a few examples has helped you understand how to make good use of The Difference Procedure. Now, let's move to learning how to identify and readily access your Optimal Mental State.

THE 5 INGREDIENTS OPTIMAL MENTAL STATE EXERCISE

Mental States are vital to our functioning, but can feel elusive. The 5 Ingredients Optimal Mental State Procedure shows us we can identify, access and stabilize our Mental States. In addition to identifying 5 important elements that comprise your OMS we will be learning about Anchoring. I learned about Anchoring in my NLP training. Based on principles of classical conditioning pairing elements helps them become associated with each other. If I press my thumb when I am Relaxed, and they become paired, I can later press my thumb and experience the Relaxation. This is amazing! It means our MS don't need to be totally out of our control. We can access them through anchoring. Now, let's get some practice identifying your OMS through the 5 Ingredients

Optimal Mental State exercise, along with practicing establishing anchors for the OMS as a way to retrieve it:

1. Think of 5 ingredients that will make up your Optimal Mental State. (There is no magic to the number 5. It just tends to work well to arrive at a fully experienced, well functioning mental state. If a different number works for you that is fine.)

2. Order the mental states in order of access, not order of importance. Order them 1-5.

3. Starting with ingredient #1, remember or imagine having best levels of this ingredient. Experience it fully. See, hear, and feel it. Picture it vividly. Now, bring that MS into the moment, adjusting your mind, body, breathing, posture, breathing, and inner voice to coincide with this ingredient.

4. Now let's experience ingredient #2. Remember or imagine this ingredient fully.....Now bring this ingredient fully into the present, adding it to #1. What do you add as you add this ingredient...breathing, inner voice, posture, energy...etc

5. Let's go to ingredient # 3. Remember or imagine this ingredient fully.....Bring this ingredient into the present.....etc

6. Time to experience ingredient # 4. Remember or imagine it fully...Bring it into the present, adding it to 1,2 and 3.

7. Experience ingredient #5. Remember or imagine having this ingredient fully...Bring it into the present, adding it to the other ingredients. What do you add?

8. As you add ingredient #5, and experience all 5 ingredients, press 2 fingers together in a unique way...Now you can let that go. (The 2 fingers pressed together are a kinesthetic anchor. By pairing the fingers with the experience of the 5 ingredients, the fingers become part of the experience. Operating like classical conditioning, you now have a quick way to access the full

Optimal Mental State. When you press the fingers in the same way, you retrieve the experience.)

9. We will now repeat the process, but a little quicker. Go through steps 3-7. At step 8, this time come up with a color or image that represents the full Optimal Mental State. (This is a visual anchor.)

10. Repeating the process once more, even quicker, go through steps 3-7. At step 8, come up with a word, phrase or sound that represents the state. (This is your auditory anchor.)

11. To check how the anchors are working, you can take a 30 second break, and then introduce the kinesthetic, visual and auditory anchors again to discover how well you retrieve the Optimal Mental State. If needed you can pair the anchors with the experience again to establish the anchors better. You may also discover that certain anchors work better for you. It is also possible to access the OMS by going through the 1.2.3.4.5 experiencing of the ingredients again. The goal is to have ways to access your OMS.

What did you discover about your Optimal Mental State and how your anchors worked?

QUICK FIXES FOR MENTAL STATE ADJUSTMENTS

Part of our Self Coaching involves our being able to monitor and adjust our MS as needed. If you are playing and you notice your Relaxation lowering, your task is to assess what is going on and problem solve it in the moment. The One Line MS is a way to assess it. Imagine putting all your individual MS on a 10 point scale. Perhaps you want each MS at a 7 or above. In that case, if an individual MS is suddenly below a 7, your task is to appreciate noticing it and access resources (like Mental Skills and Perspectives) that will move the individual MS back up to where you would like it. Using the NLP Outcome Frame, you can have: Present State = lowered Relaxation, Resources = Mental Skills of calm muscles, picture hitting relaxed; think of Perspective: Focusing on the Process, don't Worry About the Outcome; Desired State = Relaxation back at 7 or above.

The One Line MS

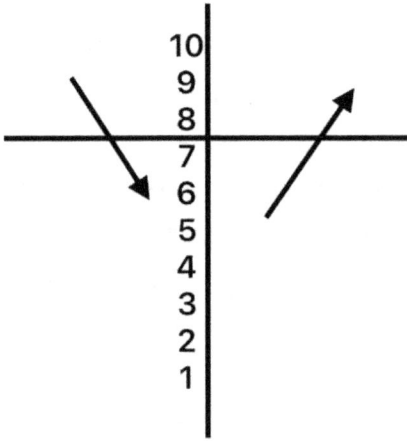

You can experience a combination of your MS as one MS. If you place all the ingredients for your MS on one line, then you could monitor whether there is a disruption of any MS. If you experience your MS as a positive combination of Relaxation, Confidence, Concentration and Confidence, and the other core states, where all tend to be above a 7 or 8 on a 10 point scale when playing ok, you can monitor if any one MS or several MS drop below the 7 (or whatever number you decide on). Below are some quick adjustments to know about:

Quick Mental State Adjustment Possibilities

1. Motivation—If there is disruption in Motivation, in the sense of "I want", you can assume some disconnection has occurred with goal setting. As such, reconnecting with goals is a good idea.

2. Confidence—If there is a disruption in Confidence, in the sense of "I can", it can help to reconnect with your performance skills through "imaging with repetition."

3. Relaxation—If there is a disruption in Relaxation, your sense of inner calm, you can loosen up your muscles with muscle relaxation, or do comfortable belly breathing, while using a soothing voice, or picturing something comfortable. Rather than do a relaxing Mental Skill, you could also think of a relaxing Perspective, such as "Do What You Know', or "Focus on the Process, Don't Worry About the Outcome".

As you mentally operate, as with the examples just noted, you are attempting to raise your MS ingredient back up to 7 or 8, or whatever level you set.

SELF COACHING AND PAR, FLOW, AND THE TRANSCENDENT PEAK EXPERIENCE/PEAK PERFORMANCE

When you do effective Self Coaching you are apt to more reliably play the way you know, which is playing up to PAR. (See the PAR chapter later for more on this.) You will have less underperforming, and more being in the flow state, where your racquet feels like part of your hand, your timing is really good, and you play enjoying the challenge, with fine concentration and enjoyment. Your results will tend to be better playing like this, but you do it for the experience for its own sake. If you are fortunate you may enter a transcendent state. I recall three such experiences.

In 1986, when Phil Landauer and I won our first USTA national tournament, the 35&over National Grass Courts, we played the #1 seeds in the quarterfinals: John James and Gene Scott. They were clearly excellent players. I had heard John James had once had a win over Bjorn Borg, and Gene Scott had played Davis Cup. At one point in the match, time slowed to a standstill for me. I remember thinking how easy and natural things were for me at that moment. There was no way I could miss, since I could put the ball anywhere I wanted. That experience was only for one point, but was memorable. The rest of the match Phil and I played really well, and won, but that point was special.

Another experience I had once was when I tried to hit a ball in practice that was on the other side of the court. My brain somehow locked onto the ball, like a plane with a bomb can lock onto a target. I hit the ball squarely. Those two experiences provide us with a window into the meta qualities and brain powers potentially available to us. There is a mystical quality to the transcendent. I believe our positive Self Coaching, which helps us be in our Optimal Mental State, increases our chances of being in flow and the transcendent zone.

A third experience occurred in 2004 when Larry Turville and I were playing in the finals of the 55&over ITF World Championships against the team of Alvarez and Riggs, in Perth, Australia. They were a really formidable team, having won the ITF World Championships previously. Lito Alvarez had played his collegiate tennis at UCLA and had played Davis Cup for Argentina. Riggs was a terrific tennis pro from Australia. Turville and I lost the first set pretty handily. Enough so that my wife, Rayna, and close friend and other doubles partner, Phil Landauer, who were watching, later said they felt sorry for me. After the first set we seemed to be in trouble. Turville asked if I wanted to change serving sides. I was serving into the wind and having trouble holding. The problem was that that would mean we would be serving on the wrong sun side. So I said, "No, let's keep these serving sides. I will go for my serve more, and we will stop going I formation to the deuce side", since that wasn't going great. They were so good, though, that I knew I had to pick up my game some way. Usually I would go inside my mind to let go and allow my inner positive Unconscious to help me let go and play my best. I didn't feel that would do it in this case. I decided to ask for a bigger power in the Universe to help. So this was felt like praying to a Higher Power. Wouldn't you know it. Suddenly all my perceptions changed, and my timing became impeccable. I didn't miss a ball the remainder of the match, and we won in 3 sets. Letting Riggs know how good a team I thought they were after the match, he told me I had been the best player on the court. What a turnaround in that match. To me, that shows the power and possibilities of the transcendent!

MY MENTAL STATE (MS) NOTES

Please use this page to answer the following questions and write down important things you understand about how your MS operate. Also, what questions do you have about your MS?

1. What Mental States are key for me? Which MS are most important for me?

2. How do my MS change between my positive and negative performances?

3. How do my Mental States work? Is there a Mental State Sequence I notice?

4. What is my Optimal Mental State? Does my OMS change for different events? How?

5. How can you access your OMS?

6. How can you adjust your mental states when needed?

7. What do you need to do to get better at managing your mental states? What is the improvement plan you can commit to?

MENTAL STATE PLAYING INVENTORY

Managing our Mental State (MS) is a vital part of Self Coaching Tennis. As such, we can give special attention to how we are doing with our MS. We can think of it as playing Mental State Tennis as well as Self Coach Tennis. As such, let's focus on doing a good job managing our MS, having that be an important process goal. The Self Coaching Tennis (SCT) Rating Scale, found elsewhere in this training, is a tool for monitoring how we are doing with our Self Coaching across the board of tasks. The Mental State Playing Inventory is a way to zoom in more on how we are doing with our MS while playing specifically.

MENTAL STATE PROFILE: We will here be rating Mental State relevant issues on a 10 point scale, where 10 = best, and 1 = worst. At times you will be asked to describe what was going on in terms of your mental state experience and playing.

1. Let's begin by assessing your MS while playing today with your Mental State Profile today. Please rate your Mental States while playing today/or for a certain event. Use a 10 point scale, where 10 = best, optimal level of a mental state, and 1 = low, worst level. After listing and rating the Core Mental States, there is room to add other mental states that you deem important, like Energetic, Playful, Fierce, or other words that you feel most importantly describe how you played. If you have very high levels of a MS, but think it got you in trouble, you can add a (+), like 10+, to indicate overconfidence, too relaxed, etc)

   Relaxed _____

   Concentration _____

   Confidence _____

   Motivation _____

   Determination _____

   Enjoyment _____

   Patience _____

   Imperturbable (Unbothered by things) _____

   Other _____ _____

   Other _____ _____

   Other _____ _____

2. Please describe what you notice about your MS Profile for this event. Are there MS that seemed especially high or low? Did it seem like a certain MS was important to getting the rest of the mental states to go up or down? Anything else you notice?

3. Rate your MS in general today _____

4. I accessed a positive MS to start the match _____

5. I maintained a positive MS throughout the match _____

6. I made adjustments to my MS as needed during the match _____

7. Please describe anything important you notice about your ability to access, maintain and adjust your MS through this event.

PLAYING LEVEL SCALE

Our Mental State Profile gives us a sense of how our mental states are operating during a match, with an indicator of how optimal/positive our MS is. We can also look at our Playing level, where we give ourselves a rating of how On or Off our game we are for the event. I believe our task is to Self Coach so that we get to at least a PAR level. The concept of PAR, coming from golf, is that if we do the basic skills of the game effectively, we will score a par on the whole. So, if we know how to play well, and hit the shots we already know, we play at a par level. What if your level of tennis, though, does not include being able to hit all shots effectively and with repetition? In the PAR approach to tennis, when rating our level of play today, we realize our task is to do what we are currently capable of doing. We can set an improvement plan to raise our level of play for the future, but our task in today's event is to play at our PAR level at this time. Your PAR level isn't just the average of how you play, because you may be underperforming in events. Your PAR level is based on a reasonable assessment of how you know how to play now. If I can consistently hit 6 out of 10 backhand returns in the court in practice and practice sets, I am at my PAR if I do that in a match. We are checking on whether you are ON Your game now. Not underperforming. The premise is that if we do effective Self Coaching, we can increase our chances of playing up to PAR. Since effective Self Coaching puts us in an optimal mental state, we also create conditions for playing even better than PAR, in a flow state, and may even on occasion get into a zone of peak performance/experience.

In the Playing Level Scale, a 6 point scale, we are way OFF our game at 1, not terrible but still underperforming at 2, pretty ok at 3 but not quite doing what I can do, and ON at 4, which is our PAR. We are even more On at 5, which is in a flow state, and 6, which is transcendent zone of peak experience/performance. Getting to a 6 is special, but tends to be rare, so we could look at this as primarily a 5 point scale. The hope is that with effective Self Coaching you can very much reduce playing at a 1 or 2, and increase times you can play at a 4 or better more consistently. So, here is the Playing Level Scale:

PLAYING LEVEL SCALE: Please rate your playing level for this match or practice on basically a 5 point scale, but allow for a 6 for extraordinary occasions:

1 = OFF—way off my game, mental state disconnected—could be tense, unfocused, unconfident, unmotivated, discouraged, frustrated or angry

2 = UNDERPERFORMED—underperformed, but not the worst I could play; playing below average, but not terrible—maybe a little tight, less than fully confident, didn't miss every shot, but inconsistent, without best timing, maybe a bit frustrated or discouraged

3 = PLAYING JUST OK—playing ok, but know I can play better; play seems average, but not my best; can make some ok shots, but don't have full timing; may have some motivation, but not fully confident, comfortable and focused

4 = ON—ON PAR—on my game; mental state positive; feeling relaxed, confident, focused, motivated and enjoying, with good energy

5 = ON—Flow state—everything clicking automatically; racquet feels like part of me; in the moment fully, embracing the challenges with positive energy and mental state: relaxed, confident, enjoying, and focused

6 = IN THE ZONE—peak experience; peak performance—may have some extra positive transcendent experience—perhaps things seem to slow down, so can't miss; experience something extra special, something extraordinary

My Playing Level for this match/practice/event = _____

If your playing level varied a lot throughout a match you can give yourself more than one score. If, for example, you played awesome the first 2 sets, which you split with your opponent, and then your playing level dropped dramatically in the 3rd set, with physical state, mental state and strokes declining, you might give yourself a 4 for the first 2 sets, and a 2 for the 3rd set.

You might give yourself between a 3 and 4 for the whole match, but that wouldn't tell the whole story. In this example, you can rate this way:

My Playing Level for the first set = _____
My Playing Level for the second set = _____
My Playing Level for the 3rd set = _____
My Playing Level overall for the match = _____

We can take the information from our Mental State Profile and our Playing Level Scale to understand how our mental states are operating when we play well and less well. We can determine what to key on in a match as well as what elements of our mental states need work for improvement. Based on your latest playing, what do you want to key on next in your play?

Chapter 7

Self Coaching: The Tennis Performance Categories

To be an effective Self Coach it is helpful to have good communication between the Self and Self Coach. It is also important to have an experience organizing model, like the NLP Outcome Frame, to help you clearly process what is going on. Having positive Self Coaching Perspectives to draw on can enable you to be in a good frame of mind. We have also done Mental Skills and Mental State training to help you further learn how to maneuver with your experience to reach your desired outcomes. You can apply the above self coaching models, perspectives and skills as you apply them working with your Tennis Performance Categories. Here, in this chapter, we will orient to the Self Coaching Performance Categories (also here called Tennis Performance Categories) you need to monitor to coach yourself. Knowing these categories and being able to monitor and work with them well can help you perform well and have a good experience. These Performance Categories include your Mental State, Performance Skills (Strokes), Game Plan/Strategy, Physical State, Relationship State and your Equipment and Environment. Beyond these Tennis Performance Categories there can be important Personal/Psychological Issues that may impact your experience and performance. To briefly describe them here:

IDENTIFYING THE TENNIS PERFORMANCE CATEGORIES

Mental State refers to the mind-body-emotion-behavior state you are in while you play and move through the world. This includes qualities like Relaxation, Confidence, Concentration, Motivation, Determination, Enjoyment, Patience and Imperturbability. There are endless possible nuances to your possible mental states that have you in various amounts of playfulness, fierceness and tenderness, or other qualities. Certain qualities and levels of those qualities facilitate your playing and experience better than others. In Self Coach Tennis one important goal is to learn how to access and maintain an Optimal Mental State. The assumption is you tend to play better and have a better experience when in a positive state. It can be challenging to do this through the vagaries of match play.

Performance Skills in tennis refers to your Strokes. We have a variety of strokes to develop and learn to become an effective player: forehand, backhand, serve, returns, volleys, lobs. Tennis is a skill sport. There is a lot of technique to master if you want to become a good player. Technique not well developed may have a tendency to break down under stress. The goal is to be able to employ the strokes you have developed during competition.

Strategy/Game Plan: We want to play smart. This involves being able to select a workable game plan that you can implement as well as tailoring your game plan and shot selection to your opponent. How does your opponent handle high backhands? Can your opponent move well to a drop shot? Do you even have a drop shot? Are you trying shots you haven't developed yet? What is your Plan A game plan? Are you a steady baseline player by nature, or a serve and volleyer? Think of yourself as Sherlock Holmes on the tennis court and tennis as like a chess game. I am older and don't move like I used to. I joke with my friends that tennis is like chess, but less running. I have had matches where changing my game plan midway through the match really made a difference. I recall one match against an excellent player where I thought I played well the first set playing my serve and volley attacking game, but lost the set handily. For the second set, then, I switched to more of a junk game, with lots of drop shots and lobs, and, to my surprise and delight, my opponent struggled with that, and I ended up winning the match. How are you at selecting and adjusting your game plan?

Physical State refers to what is going on physically. This can include your physical talents such as speed, endurance, strength and flexibility, as well as your physical health (sick or well) and injury possibilities. Tennis can be physically demanding. We need to be able to develop and employ our physical talents at whatever level they are at, as well as manage whatever health and injury issues emerge. Monitoring your Physical State effectively in a match is critical since issues with hydration, fatigue and nagging injuries can readily occur. There is also the factor of getting our bodies ready to play. How often do you start playing a match not really physically ready? Do you have a warm up routine?

Relationship State Issues: How are you at managing your relation-ship with your opponents, teammates, coaches, family, audiences? Do you get intimidated by opponents who are really good players, or not being nice? Do you get thrown off by their bad line calls? Are you in conflict because your coach wants you to play one way and you want to play another way? Do you have a parent who cares about your play but seems too critical, and that upsets you? It is important for you to be able to mange your relationship issues. That will help you clear your mind and free you up to play your game.

Equipment and Environment: Equipment is something to attend to if you want to play your match. First of all, did you remember to even bring your racquet? Did you check whether your strings were ok or about to break? Are your strings at a string tension you want? Before I played a match at the USTA National 35's Indoors in St Louis many years ago, I gave my racquet to the stringer. I was only liking playing with that one racquet (bad idea), so I told the stringer I needed the racquet for my match the next day. When I picked up the racquet, the stringer said, "Sorry. The racquet slipped while I was stringing it." I didn't really know what that meant. I went to my match. I then found out what that meant when I served and volleyed on my first point and my volley hit the tarp at the back of the court. I guess the strings were way too loose. I hit a lot of aces that day, but couldn't play in the points at all and lost badly. We need to have our racquets ready. I have also had the experience of putting on a new grip, only to find my timing off. Re-gripping it helped a lot. Our Equipment also includes shoes, braces, tape, tennis gloves (in my case), clothes, water jug, and whatever else you might need. Are you ready with your Equipment? The Environment is also important to manage. Are you ready for the temperature, whether hot or cold? Can you handle the conditions, whether windy, dark out, or a bright sun? You can see how it is important to be able to coach yourself to handle your Equipment and the Environment.

Mental Skills: Our mental skills are the sensory resource tool that help us navigate all the Tennis Performance Categories. This includes our positive self talk, positive imaging, using our capacity to visualize to mentally rehearse playing our best, and mentally rehearsing coping with potential adversity and distractions. It includes using our breathing, muscle relaxation, movement, postures and behaviors to help us. Are we focusing our self talk toward facilitating movement towards our Desired State, or more being upset and lamenting our Present State?

Personal/Psychological Issues: Psychological conditions such as depression, other mood disorders, anxiety disorders, PTSD, and ADHD can affect your ability to have the best energy and clarity to handle the stresses of playing tennis. Having low self esteem can make it difficult for a player to believe in themselves enough to compete effectively. Having relationship issues with an opponent may cloud judgment enough to impact focus on the match. Psychological treatment, such as counseling or medication, can be indicated and helpful in working through personal issues. In the meantime we can do our best to assess and problem solve our personal issues. Our Self and Self-Coach can dialogue, and using our experience organizing model, help us move toward our Desired State. We may help ourselves understand the issues and then select Self Coaching Perspectives, Mental Skills and Mental States that help. For example, being Self Accepting of our issues, we can adopt the Healthy Frame, Learning Frame, or Focus On The Process Don't Worry About The Outcome Perspective to reduce our stress and be less bothered by things when competing. Using our Relaxation and Mental State skills can also help us.

Knowing about the Tennis Performance Categories listed above provides you with a menu for monitoring what is going on while playing. The idea is if you take care of each of these Tennis Performance Categories you will tend to have a good experience and play well. Knowing about these Performance Categories helps you monitor what is going on so you can see what needs adjusting. If you don't have these Tennis Performance Categories in mind it could be harder to make sense of your experience and intervene effectively. For example, if you are missing your forehand in a match, it is helpful to know if it is a Mental State issue that needs adjusting, or a Performance Skill issue, or something else. If it is more of a Mental State issue you may be helped by doing things to help you access more Relaxation, or Confidence, or whatever the mental state issue is. If it is a technical issue, you can focus on fixing that. It also could be that it is a Physical State issue of being tired or injured, with it being difficult to set up for the shot. In that case you can hopefully appreciate that you detect whatever is going on and problem solve accordingly. Problem solving there may include hydrating or adjusting your shot to what you can currently do with your physical condition. Being Self Accepting is helpful in making all these adjustments. I like the idea of saying, "That's Ok", when something is going on on the court, like a missed shot. That is being Self Accepting. Then I use the NLP Outcome Frame to assess the Present State (missed shot), and Desired State (making the shot), and access the Resources (likely some combination of Perspectives and Skills) that will help me get me to the Desired State. To become a really good Self Coach it is important to be able to monitor your Tennis Performance Categories and be able to make adjustments in the relevant Tennis Performance Categories as needed. Monitoring and rating your Tennis Performance Categories can also help you come up with an Improvement Plan for your tennis game.

To help you monitor your Tennis Performance Categories I am now going to ask you to fill out the Self Coaching with Tennis Performance Categories Checklist. This is to give you a clear idea of what you are monitoring.

TENNIS PERFORMANCE CATEGORIES CHECKLIST
Neal Newman, Ph.D.

In order to perform well, it is important that you function well across a variety of performing categories. This includes categories such as your Mental State, Strokes, and Strategies, for example. Your task as a Self/Player and Self Coach is to monitor how well you are doing on these categories, coaching yourself to improve and perform as well as you can on each one. You can set goals for each performance, adjust during performances, and set goals for improving over time. On the following checklist you can rate from 1-10 how well you are managing each category, with 10 being best. You can rate this for your level in general on each ingredient, or you can rate the performance you just had. You can then set performance keys for the next play time, and performance goals for how you would like to improve.

114

Mental State Skills

Please rate the following on a 10 point scale, where 10 = major strength as a skill, and 1= lacking as a skill.

1. I know my best mental state. _____
2. I can step into my best mental state. _____
3. I can calm down when I need to. _____
4. I can energize/motivate myself. _____
5. I am a confident player. _____
6. I know how to boost my confidence. _____
7. I focus well. _____
8. I enjoy playing. _____
9. Nothing stops me from my best mental state. _____
10. I handle frustrations well. _____

11. What are your Mental State strengths and weaknesses?

12. Please describe your best playing Mental State, and how you access it.

13. Please identify what disrupts your best playing state, and how you deal with it.

Performance Skills – Tennis Strokes

Please rate your strokes on a 10 point scale, where 10 = very skilled, and 1 = low level of skills. You can use top players in your age group as your comparison group.

1. Forehand _____
2. Backhand _____
3. Serve _____
4. Forehand Return _____
5. Backhand Return _____
6. Forehand Volley _____
7. Backhand Volley _____
8. Overhead _____
9. Lob _____
10. Drop Shot _____

Please describe your Stroke strengths and weaknesses.

Strategy

Please rate your ability to handle strategy/game plan issues on a 10 point scale, where 10 = most skilled.

1. I know my own game. _____
2. I can design a game plan tailored to my opponent. _____
3. I can implement the game plan I select. _____
4. I can see patterns, and revise my game plan as needed. _____
5. I can play a forceful baseline game. _____
6. I can play a retrieving, counterpunching game. _____
7. I can play a serve and volley game. _____
8. I can play an all court game. _____

Please identify your Strategy strengths and weaknesses.

Physical State

Please rate how well developed you are on the following physical state issues on a 10 point scale, where 10 = most developed.

1. Strength _____
2. Speed, Agility, Quickness _____
3. Endurance/Conditioning _____
4. Flexibility _____
5. Timing/Feel _____
6. Health _____
7. Handling injuries/illness _____

Please describe your Physical State strengths and weaknesses.

Relationship Skills

Please rate your skills at managing relationships well while training or playing, on a 10 point scale, where 10 = most skilled.

1. Get along with coaches _____
2. Relate well with opponents/not intimidated _____
3. Cooperate well _____
4. Compete well _____
5. Handle audience/spectators well _____
6. Relate well with family about my tennis _____

Please describe your Relationship Skills strengths and weaknesses.

Environmental and External Factors

Please describe your ability to handle the following factors, where 10 = most skilled.

1. Environmental conditions (court surface, weather) _____
2. Equipment problems (break a string, string tension off, grip issues _____

Please describe your Environment and Equipment handling strengths and weaknesses.

Mental Skills

Please rate yourself on the following skills, where 10 = most skilled.

1. Ability to visualize how I want to play _____
2. Use mental rehearsal to prepare for matches _____
3. Use mental rehearsal to make adjustments during matches

   _____
4. Use positive self talk _____
5. Can draw on Self Coaching Perspectives _____
6. Can settle myself down as needed _____
7. Can guide myself effectively on the court _____
8. Can protect myself from adversity using protective devices

   _____
9. Set goals effectively.

Please describe your Mental Skills strengths and weaknesses.

Personal/Psychological Issues

Do you have any personal or psychological issues that you need to address and manage in order to play and enjoy a tennis event? Please describe.

CHAPTER 8

The PAR Approach

Self Coaching and the PAR Approach
to the Event Management Sequence

Working with the Event Management Sequence (EMS) is an important part of Self Coaching. The EMS is our indicator we need to Self Coach through a whole performance sequence: pre performance, during performance, and post performance. The PAR approach (P-A-R = Prepare, Adjust, Review) is designed to provide us with a systematic structure for moving through each component of the EMS. I also like the term "PAR" because in golf, if you hit a regular good shot, with each stroke on a hole, the course is designed for you to make "par" on each hole. When we perform, we would like to be inspired and perform exceptionally well, but we need a structure that allows us to do what we know how to do, and at least be on par with our game. We want to be able to reliably perform effectively. I like to say our task is to do what we know how to do. No pressure to be better than that. Rather, we set our sights on doing what we know, which is our par. In focusing well on that, we are apt to get in what Csikszentmihalyi calls a flow state, where it becomes possible to play extra well due to being absorbed, focused, confident, intrinsically motivated and enjoying. Being in a flow state puts us in a good process for being able to play at the high end of the level we are capable. There will be times extraordinary performances will emerge, but it starts with being present and doing what we know. The PAR approach provides us with a structure for being able to play at par. The PAR approach also applies my Self Coaching model through the performance process. Here is what PAR stands for here:

P = PREPARE: Pre-performance we need to get ourselves prepared to perform.

A = ADJUST: During performance we do our best to maintain a positive performance level, while making adjustments as needed throughout the process.

R = REVIEW: After a performance, it is helpful to positively review the performance, enjoying the experience, learning from it, and setting goals for the next performance.

PAR APPROACH TO EVENT MANAGEMENT SEQUENCE: PREPARE

Here is the outline I am suggesting we use to help us prepare systematically. It helps to know my Self Coaching model to implement this process, but the model is quickly learnable. You can prepare for a performance by 1) using the organizing models; 2) identifying the Self Coaching Perspectives you want to use to set the frame for performing; and 3) working with your Self Coaching Tennis Performance Categories to get yourself specifically ready for this performance. Let's describe each of these.

1. Use the Experience Organizing Models

We are going to decide to process our performing and experiences using the:

A. NLP Outcome Frame Model.

Present State	Resources	Desired State
Problem		Goal

We can use this model to ask where we are in the moment (our Present State or Problem), where we would like to be (our Desired State or Goal), and how we can get there (what Resources to use). If my arm is tense hitting a backhand volley (Present State), I can identify I want to be more relaxed and confident hitting the backhand volley (Desired State), and decide to image with repetition hitting a good backhand volley as a way to feel more confident and relaxed (Resource). If I prefer to think of Problem and Goal, rather than Present State and Desired State, I can be aware of procrastinating doing my writing (Problem), while knowing I would prefer to be writing freely (Goal). A Resource could then be to structure a time to start writing, and mentally rehearse writing at that time. Using this model keeps us clear about where we are, where we want to be, and how we can get there.

B. Gestalt Concepts Cycling Organizing Model

This model actually helps us sort our experience in a very similar way to the NLP Outcome Frame model. Gestalt Therapy is a process therapy that works well with experiencing in the moment. I will here mention three concepts that are foundational to Gestalt Therapy. Gestalt Therapy emphasizes the importance of Awareness, Experiment, and Contact. Awareness refers to our immediate attention to noticing where we are, noticing our sensations, feelings, behavior, etc.. We can then work with our experience by Experimenting with it. The idea is that a healthy experience ends in good Contact, a positive meeting of Self and boundary. In the example above, where I was feeling tense hitting a backhand volley, I would first be Aware of being tense. Then I might notice where and how I tense. I could experiment with letting go of the tension or increasing it. I could discover what happens if I attack the ball rather than tightening when it comes at me. At each step of the way, I am looking for good, healthy Contact, where I fully embrace whatever I am experimenting with. Ultimately, I will see if I am able to see the ball and hit the backhand volley solidly with good Contact. After I am done with the Contact with that experience, I can look for the next experience to experience. So I can cycle through Awareness to Experiment to Contact.... to Awareness....to Experiment...to Contact... Notice how similar this is to the NLP Outcome Frame model. We can overlay them as we sort our experiences

NLP: **Present State/Problem** **Resources** **Desired State/Goal**

Gestalt: **Awareness** **Experiment** **Contact**

Both the NLP and Gestalt models provide us with an organizing model to move from where we are to where we would like to be, while exploring how to get there.

C. Self Coaching With The Unconscious

The Self and Self Coach have positive, wise, unconscious resources within that can be utilized. This is about self connection. Just like it is possible to disconnect from our strokes and tennis game, though, we can disconnect from our inner self, thereby losing connection to inner wisdom that could help us. It can be helpful to pay attention to our reactions and feelings in the moment, and to the messages we get from our dreams and symptoms. I recall Phil Landauer once had his racquet strung too tight. He felt a very light twinge in his arm, but ignored it. Two days later he had severe tennis elbow that impaired his play. Years later when his racquet felt strung too tight again he knew to not play with it that way. We can also ask our inner self, our Unconscious, for help with information and problem solving. Recall my story in a previous chapter about asking my inner self to dream me a dream of a dissertation topic. That is an example of the Conscious and Unconscious minds communicating. Similarly, when I heard the song "When You're Smiling" before the ITF World Team Championships in Turkey, I got the signal from my Unconscious about Staying In A

Good Mood through the event. That proved very helpful. There, my Unconscious gave me a message, and my Conscious Self needed to get the message and apply it. We get signals from our feelings all the time, telling us we are variously tense, frustrated, distracted, discouraged, angry, impatient, motivated, happy, confident or enjoying. We need to listen to our feelings and decide whether to adjust or continue as is. We get signals from our body, telling us we are or are not warmed up, whether we are tired or dehydrated, or whether we have some kind of injury. We need to pay attention. The Experience Organizing Model chapter also speaks to other ways to draw on inner resources, like using ideomotor, mirroring hands approaches to get information and do problem solving. Or we can just sit quietly and ask our inner selves a question and patiently see what emerges.

Ernest Rossi in his book, *The Symptoms Path to Enlightenment,* speaks about our natural healing and problem solving that occurs by going inside and asking a question. If we are patient, we may go through a series of reactions, that may include sensations, feelings, thoughts, images, and symptoms, until we arrive at a place of insight that can help guide us. Our Conscious Self takes it from there to determine what is useful and how to utilize it to move forward. You can, for example, ask your inner self what you need to add to your preparation routine to be more ready to play at the beginning of a match. Or you can ask your inner self what you are needing to do at this time to improve your level of play. The answers we get from within sometimes just confirm what we have been thinking and provide valuable support. At other times, we may get a surprising, creative idea that provides us with a new direction we hadn't thought of yet. That was the case with my dissertation idea dream. I am older now, with my movement not optimal due to some physical issues. As I go inside to ask my inner self how to improve this, I get some ideas about movement exercises that could help. At other times, I have gotten messages about setting movement limits when trying to play safely through injuries that included a herniated disc and hamstring strain. The important issue is that we stay connected to our inner self. Our Self and Self Coach, working together, can work with their unconscious, inner wisdom to help get ideas that can be helpful.

2. Select Self Coaching (SC) Perspectives for the performance

The SC Perspectives set the frame or bigger picture around which we are performing. There are certain useful ways of thinking that help us orient ourselves to performing in a way that enhances our experience, facilitates our functioning, and helps us be the person we want to be while performing. As you prepare for an event it helps to select the positive Perspective(s) that will help you perform/play the way you want. Below is a list of SC Perspectives that seem wise in helping us maintain a useful frame that constitutes a context for our performing. This list of Self Coaching Perspectives is described in more detail in the chapter on Self Coaching Perspectives. Here they will be briefly listed. Refer to that chapter if you want more detail. This is not an exhaustive list, but rather a beginning menu to draw from.

List of Self Coaching Perspectives

1. **Learning Frame**: In the Learning Frame you give yourself a chance to experiment and develop, so you can be tolerant and patient about mistakes.

2. **Opportunity Frame**: Here you look for the opportunity in any circumstance. Rather than be depressive about life adversity, you see how one door that closes can mean another door can open.

3. **Challenge vs Threat Frame**: Relishing the Challenge in an event places you in a resourceful, eager place. If feeling threatened by the possibility of losing, or not doing well, it is easy to be too tight.

4. **Healthy Frame:** Most of us have a sense of what would be healthy and mature in an event. Committing to be healthy is apt to help us make good choices that help our experience and performance, and help us feel good about how we are being as a person.

5. **Commit to Staying in a Good Mood:** This frame helps us enjoy our experience and not be upset so readily.

6. **Self Acceptance:** Self Acceptance includes our appreciating our strengths and accepting our limits. It is part of being empathic and supportive of ourselves. Being Self Accepting we can say "that's ok" when we make a mistake and move forward from there.

7. **Other Acceptance:** Being accepting of others helps us accept other's limits and proclivities, and not become so upset by their actions. Being empathic of others can also be part of being the kind of person we want to be.

8. **Curiosity Frame:** Here we are interested in what is going on. This can help our motivation, patience and energy. Also, feelings are information. If curious about that, rather than be upset about certain reactions, we can appreciate what we detect, and get interested in what that means for us and how to best proceed.

9. **Focus On The Process; Don't Worry About The Outcome:** This Perspective allows us to attend in the moment to our process rather than tighten up from worry about the outcome. This helps us stay present.

10. **Do What You Know:** Just doing what you know takes the pressure off of thinking you somehow need to be better than you are. This is doable, and helps you focus in the moment.

11. **Possibility vs Probability Perspective:** Knowing your probability is high for doing well in an event can be comforting. Here, though, we see that we can also have a positive way

to focus when there is a Possibility for success. Our sense of possibilities can keep us focused in some positive way in the present.

12. **Focus On Your Performance Keys**: This speaks to the helpfulness of deciding where to place your focus during an event.

13. **In Training**: Having the sense of being In Training can help you make good choices, whether that involves diet, training, practicing, or developing in any way. When In Training, you might not eat all 10 cookies on a plate, and you will wake up early to train.

14. **Self Connection**: Working With Your Inner Unconscious Resources: This is a reminder to tune into our inner wisdom and communication from within, in the form of reactions, images, feelings, thoughts, sensations, and dreams, for awareness and problem solving, and to appreciate the automaticity that frees us up during play. Much of our difficulties occur with a loss of self connection, so tuning into our inner resources is important.

The above Self Coaching Perspectives provide us with a menu of wise Perspectives to draw on when about to do a performance. It would be unfair to ask you to be an effective Self Coach without providing you with an idea about the kinds of Self Coaching Perspectives that are useful and enable you to have a positive frame of mind. These Self Coaching Perspectives are useful wherever you are in the Event Management Sequence, whether preparing, adjusting during play, or reviewing your play. In the PAR Approach to Preparing to play, for example, we use an organizing model, like the NLP Outcome Frame Model, to determine where we are, how we would like to play, and how to get there. Knowing how we want to play, we prepare by selecting the wise SC Perspectives we want to keep in mind as we perform, as our context. These wise SC Perspectives constitute Resources that ready us to perform well. The list above provides you with a varied host of perspectives to use, but feel free to add to the list. Once we have identified our SC Perspectives we want to keep in mind, our task is to Prepare the Self Coaching (SC) Categories.

3. Prepare the Self Coaching Tennis Performance Categories

The Tennis Performance Categories form the content we need to take care of while performing. This includes our Mental States, Performance Skills, Game Plan and other categories. To prepare to perform, we need to determine how we want to play and get ourselves in position to do that. When we prepare well with our Tennis Performance Categories, we increase our likelihood of effective performing. Our task as Self Coaches is to prepare, monitor and adjust our Tennis Performance Categories as needed during an event. Let's now take a look at the Self Coaching Categories, looking at what they are, along with ideas for how to prepare to perform.

Mental States (MS): How we feel inside, our mind-body state, is vital to our performance experience and effectiveness. We support, energize and direct our experiences via our MS. You can select and access your full Optimal Mental State for an event (your combination of states, such as Relaxation, Concentration and Confidence combined) or decide on an Individual Mental State (eg. Enjoyment, Determination) you want to especially key on, or do both. To access your Mental State you can mentally rehearse it or use anchoring to access it. (See the Mental State chapter for how to use anchoring.). I find it helpful to briefly mentally rehearse my playing a few days ahead of time, briefly mentally rehearsing a couple of times/day. That seems to help me be especially ready. Don't just think about the mental states conceptually. It helps to experience the Mental States in an embodied way, feeling them and experiencing the postural, movement, behavioral and feeling elements of the Mental

States, as well as the cognitive component. You can check that you have accessed your Desired State when you begin the match. If you are not in the Mental State you want, you can determine what ingredients need to be added. For example, if Relaxation needs to be added you can do belly breathing or muscle relaxation, or picture yourself playing relaxed. If you are not feeling Motivated you can remind yourself of your goals for the match. If your Concentration is disrupted, you can remind yourself where you want your focus. To pick up your Determination, you can commit to your fierceness and resolve. If your Confidence is down, you can remind yourself how you know how to play and image playing effectively. For enhancing Enjoyment, you can tune into your joy for the game. If you prefer, you can also re-access your combination of mental states that comprise your Optimal Mental State. Those are a few ideas about how to help yourself access and experience your Mental States for a match.

Performance Skills (PSk): The PSk are the fundamental skills of the game. To prepare your strokes for a match, you can mentally rehearse them until you feel a connection to them. I find it very helpful to image with repetition. If, for example, you are experiencing your backhand as a 5 (on a 10 point scale, where 10 = high), you can image hitting your backhand over and over. After picturing 9 or 10 of them you might find you are now at a 7 or 8. The number you need to connect to the stroke may vary. I suggest you see the ball come at you and feel yourself hitting the ball. You can just picture this in your mind fully, or can do body rehearsal, where you are actually moving your body, swinging like hitting the ball as it comes to you. One strategy is to first see yourself hitting it "just right" and then feel yourself hitting it the way you want. You might consider taking a little time before a match to connect to each of your strokes through imaging with repetition. I have found that if I connect to my strokes using imaging with repetition before a match, the number of repetitions it takes me to connect later in the match tends to be less. It might take me 10 repetitions before, and only 2 or 3 later. A positive reminder is also to "stay with technique" with each stroke.

Strategy (Game Plan): Strategy involves your game plan for the performance. You can mentally rehearse your desired plan of action for a match. Is your Plan A game to serve and volley, be a baseliner or play an all around game? I have found it helpful to picture how I want to play a few days ahead of the match, if possible. You can also tailor your match to your opponent. Does she not move forward well, so you want to bring her forward with short shots or drop shots, and then lob or pass? Does your opponent not do well if you give him high shots to the backhand? Can you tailor your game to your opponent? Are you clear about your game plan, and flexible enough to change it when you need to? You can prepare yourself to play a certain way, and to be ready to shift it as things emerge during the match. You can also keep in mind the Hit to Advantage model. In this model, you hit to Advantage where possible, try to at least stay Neutral with your shots, and limit hitting to Disadvantage where possible. You can hit to advantage by hitting solid, moving your opponent around, or hitting to places that exploit their weakness.

Physical State (PhyS): Our PhyS includes physical skills such as speed, quickness, agility, endurance, strength, flexibility, coordination and timing. It also includes our health, injury, and wellness issues, as they impact our PhyS skills, MS and strokes. We help prepare our Physical State by training to be in shape, and eating and sleeping well. Being healthy with our wellness and training habits can help us stay healthy and be of help in avoiding injury. Eating at the right time before a match can make a difference. Being well hydrated can help. At match time, you can prepare your Physical State by doing a set of exercises that warm you up and ready you to play at full go at match onset. It is a good idea to have a routine of exercises you do that warms up your muscles and joints, so you can move and hit solid when the match begins. I feel like a lot of tennis players are remiss in this. Many players do a warm up that gets them a little warmed up, but not fully ready. A boxer or weight lifter wouldn't do that. They would make sure they are fully physically ready to compete. We can take a lesson from them. We want to be physically as well as mentally ready to compete. If you are sick or injured you might want to determine what you can do effectively at this time, and what you can do without worsening your condition.

Relationship State (RS): Are there any Relationship issues you have that could interfere with your match play? Do you need to work out something with your coach? Is your coach wanting you to play in a way you are conflicted about? If a junior player, are your parents doing things that distract you? Do you have difficulty handling missed calls by an opponent or umpire? Does the audience cheering for your opponent or saying things bother you? Are you intimidated by your opponent being a good player, or overconfident and lessening your focus because you don't think your opponent is very good? As you see, there are numerous Relationship Issues that can come into play to affect your play. To handle these as preparation, you can do the mental skill of coping rehearsal to imagine how you can effectively handle things that can occur. In certain circumstances, like in a conflict with your coach or parent, you might want to have a conversation to work out the conflict. If we don't problem solve our Relationship Issues, it can affect our Mental State and level of play during a match, because our energy, motivation and focus can be impacted.

Equipment and Environment: In preparing for a match, it is a good idea to check your equipment beforehand, hopefully early enough to be able to replace something if need be. This means checking things like strings, shoes, racquet, clothes, and other accessories like braces, jug, energy snack, etc.. You might find that your string is about to break or your shoes are too worn. I suggest you have a checklist to go through so you don't miss something. In terms of the Environment, knowing the court surface and the weather can influence how you prepare. You might want different shoes for clay, indoor or grass courts. Knowing the surface bounce can influence how you mentally rehearse the match. Knowing the temperature can influence the heaviness of clothes you wear. If it is very humid, you might also make sure you have something like a glove, wristbands or some accessory to help with that. If it is windy or sunny you can mentally prepare how to handle that. Your level of play can be impacted by Equipment and Environment, which is why they are included as Tennis Categories. I have even found that how I re-grip my racquet can affect my timing. I have had times my timing was somehow thrown off by how the grip felt, and re-gripping it helped.

Mental Skills: We use our Mental Skills when we navigate our experience, so it is certainly important as we prepare for our match. We do a lot of mental rehearsal, whether mastery rehearsal (picturing being at our best) or coping rehearsal (imagining coping effectively with potential obstacles) when we prepare for a match. How we talk with ourselves and picture what we say and visualize is important. I once asked a tennis player to picture playing a point against her nemesis. I saw her imagining a point. Her eyes moved side to side as she imagined a point, and then she made a negative grimace. I said you can picture it any way you want with you winning a point. She still pictured a point where she lost it. After a few tries she was able to change her image and image the possibility of playing a point effectively against this opponent. That was a start for her figuring out how to play against her. To Prepare for an event, we commit to using our Mental Skills tools in a way that helps us be at optimal places with each Tennis Category.

Personal/Psychological Issues: You may have personal or psychological issues to take care of before you play a match. Maybe you need to figure out how to play your best against an opponent who is intimidating with their manner or level of play. Your Self and Self Coach can talk with each other to select a Perspective (like Focus On Your Process, Don't Worry About The Outcome and being Self Accepting) that enables you to maintain your focus and a Mental State conducive to effective playing (think about how in the Simon Says game you maintain your concentration regardless of what is being said to try to distract you). Alternatively, you may have self esteem issues or issues to work through about fear of failing. Certain psychological issues like ADHD, Generalized Anxiety, Depressive or Mood Disorder, can affect your concentration, motivation and energy needed to play well. It may be important to get treatment and perhaps take medication while working through issues in counseling about handling stress and your mood. You can also assist yourself with your Self Coaching that helps you take the pressure off, and helps you maintain a positive outlook and Mental State. The Models, Perspectives and Skills taught in this Self Coaching Training tend to work very well. If you find you are still struggling it may be helpful to examine if there are some psychological issues getting in the way.

To be systematically prepared for an event, it is helpful to survey the SC Categories above and make sure each one is on full go as we get ready to start an event. Let's finish our section on Preparing by putting it all together with a sample practical routine before a match:

Preparation: Match/Playing PREPARATION ROUTINE

We know about the importance of the Self Coaching Perspectives and the need to have Tennis Performance Categories in good order when you play. In order to be nicely prepared to play, it is a good idea to have a system or routine in place. Is Preparation just what you do to get mentally and physically ready right before playing, or does it include time before that? If you have a tournament coming up, you probably need to check your Equipment ahead of time to make sure you have your racquets, shoes, grips and any other accessories ready and organized.

You probably need to check days ahead in order to give you time in case you need to string your racquets or get other accessories, like braces, grips, or wrist bands. You can also check the Environment, so that you have the right clothing for the weather, and can consider how to handle the wind, temperature, and court surface. I recommend you briefly mentally rehearse how you want to play (Mental State, Strokes, Game Plan), and do coping rehearsal for any adversity that can disrupt you. Before you play you can monitor whether there are any Relationship or Personal Issues to sort out before playing. You can select Self Coaching Perspectives you want to set as your frame for playing. Your warm up routine before you play can include selecting and accessing the MS you want and imagining hitting your strokes with repetition to help you get your timing. You are wanting to connect to your inner resources. This mental warm up needs to be combined with a physical warm up. You want to be physically ready to play as well as mentally ready. I think most tennis players are a bit remiss about getting physically ready. Ty Tucker, the renowned Ohio State University men's tennis coach, does a great job getting his players physically ready to play by having them hit a ton of balls at peak intensity before playing. Doing that is not always available, but we can do all kinds of stretches and movements right before playing. Here's a check for you: When you start playing are you ready to run full go, serve full go, and hit full go?

Here is a sample Pre-Match Warm Up Routine: *6 minutes*

1) Select any Self Coach Perspective(s) you want to set as your frame: Healthy Frame? Focus on your Process? Learning Frame; Stay in a Good Mood? Those are examples (1 minute). Here you can also decide if you have any Keys to focus on while playing.

2) Mentally rehearse the Mental State you want to be in. (2 minutes)

3) With the Mental State in mind, imagine hitting your strokes with repetition until you feel a good connection to your strokes. (3 minutes)

4) Do a physical warm up that gets you ready to serve fully, hit fully, and move fully. This includes whatever body exercises help you feel warmed up. Pick something systematic. You could do back stretches on the ground, then do hamstring, quad and calf stretches, then do shoulder stretches, then do physical movements side to side and up and back, for example. (6 minutes)

5) If you want, you can do 1, 2, and 3 above, while doing the physical warm up.

Here, now you come up with a Warm Up Routine you can commit to doing. Thing of it as like brushing your teeth. You do it every time.

Now that we are Prepared by selecting our SC Perspectives, and Preparing our SC Categories, we are ready to begin our performance. We are then ready to turn to the A part of our PAR approach to the Event Management Sequence: the Adjustments during the Event.

PAR APPROACH TO EVENT MANAGEMENT SEQUENCE: ADJUST

During performances we need to stay Aware and Adjust as necessary. If we have Prepared just right and can maintain our playing well, we just keep going, and need not mentally operate to change anything. We continue to use the NLP Outcome Frame Model, being Aware of our Present State, determining our Desired State, and accessing whatever Resources we need to reach our Desired State. We can monitor that we are maintaining the SC Perspectives we have chosen. If we need a reminder about our selected SC Perspectives we can do that. I can remind myself to Focus on my Process, and not worry about the outcome. I can remind myself to face the Challenge, or be in a Learning frame. If I want to add in another SC Perspective I can do that. Staying in a Positive Mood could be important to emphasize. As the event proceeds, I monitor my SC Categories. If I miss a shot in tennis, did I break technique (PSk problem), was I distracted by something (MS disruption), was it an ineffective way to play the point (Strategy issue), or was I just tired and dehydrated (PhS problem)? Our task is to be self aware, so that we can make an Adjustment in the relevant SC Category. Below are some Adjustments you can make in SC Categories:

- **Mental State (MS) Adjustments:** We can use our combination of mental skills and perspectives to make adjustments in our MS. If we have prepared well, we hopefully are performing with an optimal Mental State that combines positive levels of the core MS and any other ingredients deemed desirable. If in the process of performing we experience a disruption of any parts of our MS, our task is to make adjustments that help restore our optimal MS. I will now list a few MS Adjustments for specific core MS:

- **Relaxation:** If you find you are tensing up, you can use your mental skills for Relaxation. You can do belly breathing, muscle relaxation, visual imagery for inner calm, soothing voice, etc. Combining this with a perspective that takes the pressure off is often helpful in combination with the mental skills. So I can think of being in the Learning Frame, while I relax my muscles in a useful way that helps me perform the needed tasks.

- **Confidence:** Confidence is the sense of "I can". When feeling a lack of Confidence, I can remind myself when I did well before, or picture doing ok now. Also, rather than being fearful I am not good enough, I can remind myself to Do What I Know. I can be Confident in that. Imaging what I am doing with repetition can also connect me to my timing and improve my Confidence. We do not need to think of Confidence as a matter of general self esteem. Instead we can specifically think of our task, and what we know how to do. We can then do what we know with Confidence. You can also think of Confidence as a mind body state you step into. I may not know how to drive from Columbus to Indianapolis, but I could still ask for directions confidently. From within a stance of a Confidence, we are not shrinking from the event. We, instead, can behave with a sense of boldness and strength.

— **Concentration:** Concentration refers to "I focus". It helps to know where we want our attention, so if we are momentarily distracted from that, we can return our focus to where we want it. Much of Concentration disruption is exacerbated when we get upset that we are distracted, and stop focusing further. If we will allow ourselves to return to our desired focus we will find we can keep up a positive level of Concentration. Remember, Concentration involves being fully present (like concentrated orange juice contains a full amount of the juice) and knowing where we want our attention. As presence, Concentration includes a mind body state that has clear behavioral correlates. When I concentrate playing tennis, I feel energy in my eyes, and my legs have a wider base with knees bent. There is a sense of energy and alertness. As focus, we need to know what is task relevant. So, worrying whether the audience likes us in a music performance or whether we will win the tennis match is of interest to us, but may not in the moment be relevant to a full focus on conveying the music or seeing the ball to make good contact as we hit the ball. If there is an issue bothering us that is taking away our attention, we can process that quickly in the moment, knowing we can think it through further at a later time, if we want. Let us remember that a performance requires Simon Says game focus. In the game Simon Says, the player is told to only do things when the presenter says Simon Says. Easy, right? We should always win that game, but we sometimes allow ourselves to lose our focus. You decide to play with a MS of Enjoyment, Relaxation and Motivation, but lose it when your opponent makes a bad call? Once we decide where our attention needs to be to perform well, we can't allow ourselves to be suckered out of that focus. John McEnroe was brilliant at keeping his focus while distracting others at times with his antics. Brad Gilbert tells a story in his book, Winning Ugly, about playing McEnroe. Gilbert was known for being mentally tough, and finding a way to win. His goal in playing McEnroe was not to allow him to distract him from his game. They played a very close match, in which Gilbert stayed still and quiet while McEnroe spent the match questioning things, complaining and delaying the contest. As it got to the end of the match, at a key point in the match, Gilbert went to towel off. It was a very hot and humid day. McEnroe immediately said to the umpire how terrible it was how much time Gilbert was taking, and the umpire issued Gilbert a warning. Gilbert, who had been so quiet and well behaved all the match, while McEnroe had been the one delaying things, got incensed, lost focus and lost the match. Later on, at a player event, McEnroe complimented Gilbert for a fine match but, with a twinkle in his eye, told him he just needs to watch his delaying things.

— **Motivation:** Motivation is the sense of "I want". When you hear the language of a performer saying he or she doesn't want to participate, you know Motivation is involved. A loss of Motivation is a loss in connection to one's goals. To restore Motivation it is important to regain connection to one's goals. To do this you need to do some goal setting. Years ago I did mental training with the men's swim team at Ohio State University. The swimmers worked hard. The training was impressive and grueling, with early morning wake-up to train the norm. It wasn't unusual for a swimmer to question their participation and consider quitting. Typically, though, when they reminded themselves of their swimming goals, including the swim times they wanted to achieve and how they wanted to place at the Big 10 meet, and they found ways to have their training feel relevant, they stayed on the team, experiencing their commitment once again.

— **Enjoyment:** Enjoyment refers to the sense of "I like". For some people, with a stringent work ethic, Enjoyment may not seem pivotal to performance, but many performers do find Enjoyment essential. For some performers, without Enjoyment, they don't even want to be there (meaning without Enjoyment they lose Motivation). Enjoyment may then set the frame for some performers. Keeping the perspective of Enjoyment means to stay connected with the bigger picture of the joy of participating in the event. The mind body state of Enjoyment can feel light and playful, but could also involve being gritty and fully absorbed and present. When Enjoying one may find it easier to not be bothered by mistakes or adversity.

— **Patience:** Patience is a corollary to Relaxation on the space-time continuum. If Relaxation involves ability to move freely in space, without constriction and tension, Patience involves transcending time. With Patience, there is no pressure about time. As a musician being Patient, there is no hurry, and the musical line can breathe. As a tennis player, being Patient means you do not rush the point. You give yourself the time needed to set up a point. To access the MS of Patience you can mentally rehearse being Patient in your event. Doing the mental skill of slow belly breathing to a count of 5 you can also slow down your personal tempo, which helps increase your Patience.

- **Performance Skill (PSk) Adjustments:** A performer's task is to stay with technique with their PSk. When we have PSk disruptions, I suggest we say "that's ok", followed by decoding what went wrong and then seeing what remedy we need to fix it. Sometimes a PSk disruption is actually a Mental State issue. You get tense and your movement gets tight or constricted. Or you lose motivation which affects your footwork in tennis, or affects your attentiveness to the music. At other times A PSk disruption is just that, a breakdown in your technique. This can occur when your technique isn't solid, when you pick up some bad habits, or when your technique breaks down under pressure. You can mentally rehearse your good technique as a way to tune into it. I highly recommend "imaging with repetition" as a way to re-connect with your PSk. That can work whether you have disrupted technique due to a Mental State issue, or disrupted technique due to a PSk breakdown. By the way, I have found that some performers prefer to attend to Mental States, and some prefer to attend to Performance Skills. We can do imaging with repetition focusing on either MS or PSk. One way we might focus on lessening tension and seeing how fluid the movement becomes. The other way we go directly to adjusting technique to the way we want it.

– **Strategy Adjustments (Game Plan in sports, Interpretation in Music):** A player/performer's Mental State and Performance Skills could be going fine, but performance issues can still show up if there are Strategy problems. It is important to select a Strategy and implement it. Problems can occur because a clear Strategy has not been formulated, or is not being implemented well. Adjustments during performance may be made to clarify what the Strategy is or implement it better. Alternatively, it may be important to be flexible enough to switch Strategy as needed. I recall a match years ago where I played a formidable opponent at the 35&over national Clay Courts, who later won the national grass courts. He liked pace, and when I attacked him with my serve & volley plan A game, he had no trouble. He won the first set easily. I had felt good about how I was playing, but it was clear I needed to try something else. To my surprise and delight, when I switched to a junk game of taking the pace off and hitting drop shots and lobs, he struggled. It threw off his timing. The match turned around and I won. We need to be flexible to try something else if what we are doing isn't working.

— **Physical State (PhS):** A performer's task is to do their best to access and maintain their best Physical State. To maintain one's PhS during performances, one may need to hydrate sufficiently, eat energy bars, stretch, or do other things based on the particular event. When there is a disruption in performance, this is one of the categories to monitor. Ivan Lendl was one of the top male tennis players in the 1980's. I remember sportswriters claiming he wasn't mentally tough at the beginning of his career, because he would lose some big, long matches. At a certain point he made a big commitment to his physical fitness. After that, he started winning grand slams. It turned out the issue was his Physical State, not his Mental State. Health and injury are also important to take into account as we perform. We need to appreciate our limits, given injuries and health, and do the best with what we have. If we ignore our body signals, we are apt to hurt ourselves further, leading to possible time away from our performance activity.

— **Relationship State (RS):** Interpersonal support can be helpful to performance. Others' ideas and belief in us can help us perform at our best. When I was younger, and playing a lot of basketball, I recall going to a gym, and overhearing people saying what a good shooter I was. I was a good shooter, but that day I shot particularly well. Sometimes, though, we can experience performance disruption when we feel besieged by the critical eye or statement from another, or stressed by imagined or real expectations of others, or betrayed by some form of mistreatment or unfair behavior from others. A baseball player who stops trusting the umpire's calling of balls and strikes may swing at a bad pitch believing the strike zone has been enlarged. A tennis player may feel enraged by perceived bad calls from an opponent, conflicted by disagreeing with a coach's prescribed playing strategy, or pressured by a parent's expectations. Relationship issues need to be processed and worked out, so that a person can play with a clear, aligned, focused mental state, without the distractions of a relationship conflict. We can do quick problem solving, focusing on dealing with the situation as well as possible. Sometimes we need to be more Other-Accepting, where we are empathic of others. We may realize that others can make mistakes, too, and not attribute evil intentions to them. If we do indeed not trust them, though, rather than play angrily, or frustrated, we problem solve the situation. Maybe as a tennis player we call on the umpire or tournament director if we get a number of bad calls. We may agree to disagree about certain ideas with coaches. We may allow ourselves clear boundaries with our parents, so they are allowed their expectations, while I do what I am capable of in the moment, without feeling undue pressure. In the midst of a performance, it may be difficult to think this through, but we can maintain our commitment to our Optimal Mental State, not allowing things to distract us from our commitment to our focus on playing. So, just as we move on from a mistake we make, saying "that's ok, so we move on from a mistake someone else makes, saying "that's ok." That's how we employ compassion to ourselves and others, Self-Acceptance and Other-Acceptance, along with our commitment to performance.

— **Environment & Equipment Issues:** It is important we be ready for Environment issues and Equipment issues. Sometimes the temperature in a place can affect an instrument. Or a pianist's hands may feel cold in a cold room. Certain things we know about ahead of time and certain things emerge during a performance. A tennis player's strings may suddenly break, or the strings may prove to be too loose or tight. We can do coping rehearsal prior to a performance to be ready to handle the myriad of things that can affect us with the Environment and our Equipment. The bottom line Perspective is we need to play the best we can given whatever has emerged. If my tennis strings don't feel right I can change racquets. If I put a new grip on my racquet before the match and my timing feels off, I could re-grip it. So, we can accept the circumstance, but also do whatever problem solving is possible. It is important to not allow Environmental or Equipment difficulties to disrupt our Mental State while performing.

— **Mental Skills:** During an event, it is essential we keep using our Mental Skills in a positive way. This means reacting to events with positive self talk and positive imagery. This involves keeping access to our positive Self Coach interacting with our Self. I find it helpful to use the "that's ok" response to mistakes on my part, or others. It is also important to maintain a positive problem solving perspective that comes from using the NLP Outcome Frame, and positive Perspectives, such as the Curiosity Frame, Committing to Staying in a Good Mood, Focusing on the Process, and Not Worrying about the Outcome, etc.. Using positive self talk means understanding our words impact our Mental State. As such, our task is to say things to help us be aware of our Present State, and help move us towards our Desired State. We do not want to spend our time lamenting our present plight.

To help us make Adjustments when playing tennis, it is helpful to monitor our Tennis Performance Categories. We have discussed each category separately. We can use the One Line Monitoring approach to monitoring to detect when a Tennis Performance Category is disrupted:

Match Play Adjustments Strategy: the One Line Tennis Performance Categories Monitoring:

In the Mental State Training chapter we showed how you can place all the Core Mental States on one line. If a Mental State lowers, that is your indicator to make an Adjustment to raise it. Here, we are using the One Line Monitoring to monitor the Tennis Performance Categories.

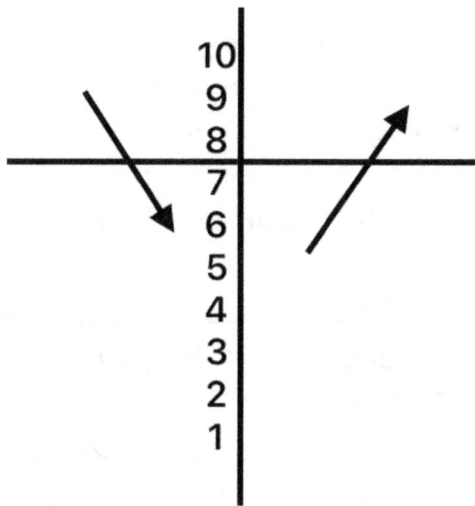

Tennis Performance Categories: Mental States, Strokes, Strategy, Physical State, Relationship Issues, Mental Skills, Equipment & Environment, Personal Issues

If your rating of any of these Tennis Categories drops during a match, your Self Coaching task is to problem solve it to make a quick fix. You move from Present State to Desired State with the Performance Category that had dropped. For example, if you become tired and dehydrated

(Physical State), you might eat an energy bar and drink fluids with electrolytes. We've seen Djokovic seem tired and out of it in a match, and then recover amazingly after eating and drinking something. In that case his Physical State may have dropped from 8 to 4 when tired and dehydrated, and raised back to 8 after eating and drinking something.

Next we will turn to the Review portion of the P-A-R approach to the Event Management with a training on the use of the P-I-E approach.

PAR APPROACH TO EVENT MANAGEMENT SEQUENCE: REVIEW

After a performance is a good time to review the performance in a positive way. This can include reviewing the positive things we did and the things we enjoyed or found interesting during the event, and the things we can learn from the performance. We can review how well our Perspectives worked for us, and can review our performance across the SC Categories. I will here propose a strategy we can use to give ourselves feedback or provide feedback to others. I call it the PIE Approach.

The PIE approach to giving self or other feedback after a performance: In the PIE Approach, P = Praise; I = Improve; E = Encourage

   — *P = Praise*: Too many people are overly harsh and self critical following a performance. I believe, however, it is healthy to review a performance for the joy as well as learning from the performance. We can start by Praising what we did. This can include the things we did well, and even include the praise of what others did well. Hopefully we can experience the joy of things done well as well as the joy of interesting and fun things that may have occurred during the performance. Reviewing the Positives also helps to reinforce the learning of doing the positives and reinforces the joy of performing.

- *I = **Improve***: In the context of the joy and praise of performing, we can then turn to the performance as a learning experience. What could I do better? What could I improve? This is done with curiosity, not chastisement. I might note I was too tentative in one place, or allowed something to bother me in another place. I might then examine the importance of being bolder in the one example, and staying unbothered and focused in the other example. Using our NLP Problem Solving model, I am here seeing the area to improve as the Present State/Problem, and translating it to the Desired State/Goal. So, if I notice I am tensing up on my backhand volley, I can identify I need to loosen up on my backhand volley. That's what needs Improving.

- *E = **Encourage***: Here we focus on Encouraging the improvement we identified as needing. To encourage the improvement is to invoke the Resources that will help us move from the Present State/Problem to the Desired State/Goal. Mentally rehearsing freeing up my backhand volley, so that I can do that next time, is an example of Encouraging the improvement to happen. With Encouraging I focus on making the improvement happen, and how to do that.

The PIE model can be used when reviewing my own performances or when giving feedback to another person on their performance. When I was doing music performance enhancement seminars, students gave their fellow students great feedback using the PIE approach. By starting with Praise and focusing on the positives of the performance, the students receiving the feedback were more open to what needed Improving. If you want to be systematic you can review the event speaking to the Self Coaching Perspectives selected or needed, and reviewing the Tennis Performance Categories.

145

PIE Approach to reviewing an event: Example

Situation: Player just lost a close 3 setter to a good player

P = Praise—what you liked, enjoyed:

>Self Coach to Self: What did you enjoy about the event, and what did you like about how you played?

>Self: That was a tough match, but fun. We had some great points. My opponent had a great shot when he ran back to chase down a lob and then hit a turnaround overhead. I thought my strokes were good, especially my forehand. I liked that I was patient setting up the points, and stayed gritty throughout the match. I also enjoyed some winners I had, like the down the line return in the 3rd set, and drop shot then lob combination I used twice.

>Self Coach: It was a fun, tough match. You were steady with your strokes, and played hard throughout. You had some fun plays.

I = Improve—what you could improve on

>Self Coach: What could you have done better?

>Self: I liked my strokes in general, but sometimes I could have gone for more, and I think I played too safe with my volleys.

>Self Coach: You were steady and gritty, but sounds like you played a little too safe, especially with your volleys.

>Self: Yes. I think I can go for more and still be stable. Too much of the time I stay Neutral in the point, but could hit more to Advantage.

E = Encourage—encourage making the improvement

>Self Coach: Sounds like to improve, you would like to stay stable but be more aggressive with your shots. Do you have a plan for how to do that?

>Self: I think I need to free myself up a bit more.

>Self Coach: How can you do that?

Self: I can picture myself hitting freely, and with more racquet speed. I have to be not so afraid to miss.

Self Coach: You would like to get in a more freed up mode. You can commit to that as a performance key, and focus on that as your process, without worrying about the outcome. That means your goal is to go for your shot the way you want to, and not worry about whether you miss.

Self: That's a good idea. Once I am in the mode of going for my shots, it will be easier to do it.

The above is an example of your Self and Self Coach working together effectively to review a match using the PIE approach.

Review Strategy

I recommend using the P-I-E (Praise—Improve—Encourage) to enjoy, learn from, and come up with an improvement plan for your play. In addition to grading your play level, and giving yourself a Self Coaching grade, you can look across each Tennis Performance Category to see how you did. I hope you will use the P-I-E approach as you review your responses to the Tennis Performance Category Checklist.

THE PAR APPROACH TO THE EVENT MANAGEMENT SEQUENCE SUMMARY

The PAR Approach is designed to take you through time with any event from before the event, to during the event, to after the event. The idea is if you follow the prescriptions for the PAR Approach, you will maximize your chances of playing up to your ability and level of development. The hope is that you will find yourself playing "on", rather than being "off". To remind you, the steps of the PAR Approach for P (prepare pre-event) and A (aware and adjusting during event) and R (review post event) are done using the following steps:

1. **Use your Experience Organizing Model:** You can process your experiences using the NLP Outcome Frame (Present State / Problem…. Resources…. Desired State / Goal) or Gestalt Concepts Cycling Organizing Model (Awareness…. Experiment…. Contact). If you have another model you want to use to filter your experience, the approach starts by making sure you are using your processing model.

2. **Select your Self Coaching Perspectives:** This is where you select your Perspectives that set the frame for you performing. Are you picking the Learning Frame, Healthy Frame, or some other Perspectives? You can adjust, change or add Perspectives during events. Post event, you can appreciate the Perspectives that helped and set Perspective goals for the next event.

3. **Monitor, Access, Adjust and Review your Tennis Performance Categories:** How are you doing with your Mental State, Performance Skills, Strategy, etc.? You want to be at optimal levels of your Tennis Performance Categories, or make adjustments to get there, or make the best with what you have. It will, for example, help you to select and access your Optimal Mental State for playing, and make adjustments as needed. Connecting to your strokes (Performance Skills) will help your timing and Confidence in your strokes. Being smart about your game plan will assist your playing greatly. You get the idea about the importance of attending effectively to your Tennis Performance Categories. When Reviewing you can appreciate what you liked about your Tennis Performance Categories while also setting Tennis Performance Categories goals for improvement. To help monitor after playing you can fill out the: 1) Mental State Playing Inventory and Playing Level Scale; 2) Tennis Performance Categories Checklist; 3) Self Coach Tennis (SCT) Rating Scale

4. **Use the P-I-E Approach for Reviewing:** When reviewing your own or someone else's performance, I recommend using the P-I-E (Praise-Improve-Encourage) Approach. That will help a person enjoy their event, cement the positives, and improve on what needs improving. Remember, when Praising what you enjoyed and did well, and when focusing on what needs Improving and Encouraging how to do that, you can be commenting on Perspectives and Tennis Performance Categories as well as the Event Management Sequence (issues related to Preparing, Adjusting and Reviewing).

Self Coaching Summary

Self Coaching Organizing Model:
1. NLP Problem Solving Model (also called NLP Outcome Frame)
2. Gestalt Concepts Cycling Model
3. Self Coaching with the Unconscious

List of Self Coaching Perspectives:
1. Learning Frame
2. Opportunity Frame
3. Challenge vs Threat Frame
4. Healthy Frame
5. Commit to Staying in a Good Mood
6. Self Acceptance
7. Other Acceptance
8. Curiosity Frame
9. Focus on Your Process, Don't Worry About the Outcome
10. Do What You Know
11. Possibility vs Probability Perspective
12. Focus on your Performance Keys

13. In Training
14. Self Connection: Working with your Inner, Unconscious Resources
15. Other:

List of Self Coaching Categories:

1. Mental States
2. Performance Skills (Strokes)
3. Strategy (Game Plan, Interpretation)
4. Physical State
5. Relationship State
6. Environment & Equipment issues
7. Mental Skills
8. Personal/Psychological Issues

PAR Approach to the Event Management Sequence:

1. Prepare
2. Adjust
3. Review (including PIE Approach)

SELF COACH TENNIS (SCT) RATING SCALE

Neal Newman, Ph.D.

The SCT Rating Scale is designed to help you monitor how effectively you are Self Coaching. This can serve as a reminder to use the models, perspectives, and skills taught in this SCT training program, and a help in guiding your practicing what you are learning. As you rate each item, you can discover what you are already using and adept at, and also see what you need to practice. The idea is to commit to SCT with your goal being to be able to masterfully work with yourself to achieve your outcomes for practicing and playing and being the person you want to be when involved in an event. Please rate each item on a 10 point scale, where 1 = no use, very low use or unhelpful use and 10

= very effective use, with the SC skill or perspective being used adroitly and masterfully.

SCT-General SC Processes—Models, Perspectives, Skills Rating (1-10, 10 = best)

_____ I understand I am both a Self/Player and Self Coach when I play tennis

_____ My Self and Self Coach are working well together to help me manage playing

_____ My Self Coach (SC) is positive, being wise, welcoming, supportive, facilitative and guiding as needed

_____ I am using an Experience Organizing Model, where I identify my Present State, set my Desired State and facilitate accessing Resources that help me get to my Desired State

_____ My SC helps Support me, being understanding, kind, patient and self accepting

_____ My SC helps Activate me to have positive energy and a positive Mental State, with positive focus, intensity, motivation and determination

_____ My SC helps Direct/guide me to be able to set goals and access resources that will help me reach those goals

SCT—Self Coaching Perspectives

_____ My SC helps me have a positive frame of mind, by drawing on useful SC Perspectives

(Like the Learning, Opportunity, Challenging, Curiosity and Healthy frames, etc)

Please list the SC Perspectives you find most useful _____

SCT—Mental Skills

_____ I am using positive self talk

_____ I am using imagery to positively affect me

_____ I am using movement, breathing, and muscle relaxation to help my mental state

_____ I use protective devices to keep me from being bothered by outside adversity or frustrations, such as plexiglass shield, force field, bubble, and step back

SCT—Mental States

_____ I understand my optimal Mental State

_____ I can access my optimal Mental State

_____ I can make Adjustments with my Mental State during a match

Please describe what you are understanding as important about your Mental State:_____

_____

_____

SCT—Tennis Performance Categories

_____ I understand where I am in terms of my Tennis Performance Categories—Mental State, Strokes, Strategy, Physical State, Relationship Management, Dealing with Environment and Equipment, Personal issues affecting playing

_____ I am managing my Performance Categories issues well during my playing times

_____ I have an improvement plan for handling my Performance Categories issues

Please describe your most important Tennis Performance Categories issues now:_____

_____

_____

SCT—The PAR Event Management Sequence

_____ I am Preparing well to play, getting myself mentally and physically ready, and readying my Tennis Performance Categories

_____ I am Adjusting my Tennis Performance Categories as needed while playing

_____ I am Reviewing my playing positively post playing using the P-I-E approach—Praise, Improve, Encourage. This allows me to enjoy the playing and set improvement goals.

SCT—Personal Issues: working through personal issues affecting performance

_____ I do not have personal issues affecting my ability to compete effectively

_____ I understand my personal issues affecting my competing and am handling them well

SCT—Goals Rating (1-10, 10 = best)

I am having a positive experience playing _____

My SC helps me play better _____

My SC helps me set improvement goals and plans _____

My SC helps me be the person I want when I play _____

Give yourself a Playing and Self Coaching grade for your practicing or playing today, where A = best, and F = worst.

Playing Grade today _____   Self Coaching Grade today _____

Describe your key points for improving your Self Coaching for the next time you play. What do you need in order to play better, and how can you coach yourself better?

CHAPTER 9

Self Coaching
With Mental Game Issues

Using our Self Coach Tennis Models, Perspectives, and Skills to manage mental game/psychological issues related to tennis performance

N ow that we have done training on Self Coaching, Experience Organizing Models, Self Coaching Perspectives, Mental Skills, Mental States, Tennis Performance Categories, and the Event Management Sequence, let's take a look at how we can coach ourselves through some common psychological and performance issues we may face when playing tennis. This is not an exhaustive list, but presented more to provide you with examples of how to use the models, perspectives and skills presented in this training. I may organize it somewhat by Performance Categories, but understand several Performance Categories are often interconnected. For example, if you are tense hitting a stroke, that could be a Performance Skill (stroke) issue as well as a Mental State (Confidence, Relaxation) issue.

PERFORMANCE SKILL ISSUE: EXAMPLE 1

Issue: Tennis Amnesia

Understanding the issue: Sometimes it can seem like we have forgotten how to play tennis. Our strokes and mental state are all off. It could be due to a number of issues. Maybe we are feeling tight, fearing losing. Maybe we are tired or sick. Perhaps we have lost focus because other things are on our mind. Regardless, it suggests a disconnection from our playing resources. I say disconnection, because we are currently not doing things we ordinarily know how to do. If we didn't know how to hit a backhand volley, and we missed one, that is not a disconnect. Rather, that would be a learning or development issue of how to hit a backhand volley.

Using the NLP Outcome Frame experience organizing model:

Present State: Tennis Amnesia—disconnected from strokes; loss of timing

Desired State: Regain connection to playing resources; be able to hit strokes

Resources: First, it would help to understand if there is an issue to process creating the difficulty. Is there a physical injury or illness affecting you, pressure you are feeling about the match, or some personal issue distracting you? You may need to process that in a self accepting way to help restore your connection to your game. There are then some Perspectives and Mental Skills we can employ to help ourselves. Certain Perspectives can support us here. First, it would help to be Self Accepting about our playing in the moment. Hopefully, that helps us be less upset. We could view it as an Opportunity to practice coaching ourselves to playing better. Focusing on the Process, rather than Worrying about the Outcome would be helpful. Once we have the positive perspectives, we could then use the Mental Skill of visualizing our strokes a number of times, until we feel more connected. "Picturing with Repetition" is a helpful mental skill to employ. If I rate my feeling for my backhand right now, as a 6/10, and I then picture hitting a backhand 8-10 times, seeing the ball coming to me in my mind, and feeling myself hitting it, I may find that I now rate my confidence in the stroke move to 8/10. How many repetitions it takes can vary.

I hope you can see in the above how we can impact our experience by using the experiencing organizing model to identify our Present State and Desired State, and use our Perspectives and Skills to access the Resources that get us our desired outcome. That is Self Coaching.

MENTAL STATE ISSUE: EXAMPLE 2

Issue: The Game Without The Game : a loss of Concentration

Understanding the issue: People talk about The Game Within The Game, referring to the mental game. There, however, is a Game Without The Game, where we lose our focus, intensity and game plan. Lots of things can conspire to take us away from our focus. Perhaps we decide to have fun moving our opponent around, rather than finish points. Perhaps we are upset with our opponent's line calls. Or maybe we are so frustrated with missing shots that we lose heart. Whatever the reason, here we have stopped playing our game.

Using the NLP Outcome Frame experience organizing model:

Present State: loss of focus; not playing our game with our game plan and mental state

Desired State: play my game with good focus

Resources: i need to remind myself of the way I want to play, and not let anything derail me from that. I think the Simon Says game is a good reminder. In this game a person is only allowed to move when the leader of the game says "Simon Says." It's a winnable game, but only if you don't allow yourself to be distracted. Similarly, in tennis you can decide how to play with energy and focus, no matter what happens with the score, your shot, your opponent, your equipment, the weather, etc. The mental state of being Imperturbable is helpful here. This is the mental state of not being bothered.

PHYSICAL STATE ISSUE: EXAMPLE 3

Issue: Anything Worth Doing Is Worth Doing Poorly—recovery from injury; learning a stroke

Understanding the issue: The saying usually goes, "Anything worth doing is worth doing well." I agree with this, in that we want to do as well as we can, putting in the time and giving our best effort. This can be perfectionistically misunderstood, where players will not play if they can't play great. If you are recovering from injury, you may need to start the road back to playing at a low level. Similarly, your level of play may be pretty low when you want to learn a new stroke. This is where, "anything worth doing is worth doing poorly.

Using the NLP Outcome Frame experience organizing model

Present State: Recovering from Injury; or Learning a stroke

Desired State: Get a chance to come back from injury and improve play; or improve a stroke

Resource: Here it would be helpful to be Self Accepting about where you are and be in a Learning Frame, to give yourself the time to come back and learn. In the case of learning a stroke, the Curiosity Frame could open you to trying things out.

MENTAL STATE ISSUE: EXAMPLE 4

Issue: Tennis Anxiety

Understanding the issue: There are many things in tennis that players worry and get tense about. You may fear losing to an opponent with a lower ranking, or someone you think you are supposed to beat. You may tighten up when ahead in a match, not wanting to blow the lead. Playing to "not miss" likely does not free you up enough to go for your shots. You may worry about not feeling confident in your strokes at a given time. We can find a way to worry about anything. This "what if….", with a negative end to the sentence, can readily tense us and impact our game.

Using the NLP Outcome Frame experience organizing model:

Present State: Worry about losing, holding lead, strokes feeling tight

Desired State: Freed up, Relaxed strokes, can play my game with good inner calm and energy

Resources: Worry seems to include some thinking about negative things occurring in the future, so Perspective wise, it helps to help yourself be present. Focus on the Process, Not Worry about the Outcome is a helpful Perspective for this. This involves focusing on your performance keys, optimal mental state, and freed up strokes. It helps to mentally rehearse these things. You can picture your strokes freed up. You can picture this from the outside, seeing yourself freed up, and you can see this from the inside, in your body, feeling the stroke as you hit it. It is also useful to use your Relaxation skills to access a freed up state. You can do belly breathing, muscle relaxation, imaging or whatever Relaxation skill or skills you find useful. Pairing Relaxation with a positive Perspective is a good idea to help you maintain your inner calm.

MENTAL STATE ISSUE: EXAMPLE 5

Issue: Tennis Confidence

Understanding the issue: Confidence is the sense of "I can". After missing several backhands, your Confidence in hitting your backhand might lessen. Or, you might be playing a tough opponent you don't think you can beat. A person may also be generally unconfident, so they go through the world generally not believing in themselves. There can also be issues on the other side, where a player is overconfident, and that affects their focus and effort.

Using the NLP Outcome Frame

Present State: lack of Confidence—hitting tight and tentative; or overconfident—unfocused and lackadaisical

Desired State: playing freely and confidently; going for shots with good energy and focus

Resources: There are several Perspectives and Skills helpful to deal with Confidence issues. One Perspective is to reframe Confidence into something specific. I don't have to be Confident in general; I can be Confident in my forehand. Another is to realize I am just wanting to be Confident in what I already have developed. I don't have to believe I can hit a forehand like Carlos Alcaraz. I can be Confident I can hit the forehand I already know how to hit. This is the Perspective of "I'm just doing what I know". I can connect to that, if needed, by the Mental Skill of "imaging with repetition". As I do that my connection to my stroke will tend to increase. If I need to develop the stroke so it is better than I currently have it, the Learning Frame and Self Acceptance will give me the time and Patience to experiment and develop. If I am not Confident in playing a given opponent, I can think of the Probability vs Possibility Frame. I may believe the probability is that my opponent is better, but it is still possible for me to come up with a game plan to give me a chance. In the case of being overconfident, it can be useful to respect your opponent by giving them your best effort. Reminding yourself of your daily goals for how you want to play and have good playing habits may be helpful. Having a goal of maintaining your optimal mental state can also keep useful. Another issue with Confidence as a Mental State is that in addition to having the sense of "I can" it can also involve a way of being. So, I may not be Confident I know how to drive to New York City from Columbus, Ohio, but I can confidently ask someone for directions. This is Confidence as an approach, as a manner of being. Having a Confident manner may help free you up enough to play in the bold, focused, connected way you want.

MENTAL STATE ISSUE: EXAMPLE 6

Issue: Frustration; Discouragement

Understanding the issue: It is not uncommon for a player to overrate their skill level on a stroke. They can hit a great topspin backhand, but they don't realize they really can't yet hit it 5 times in a row. These faulty expectations can lead to a lot of frustration and discouragement. A player can also be discouraged about some match losses.

Using the NLP Outcome Frame:

Present State: frustrated with stroke; discouraged about match loss

Desired State: feel good about working on and hitting the stroke; feel good about figuring out what is going on in the matches and working on improving.

Resources: With frustrations about strokes, it helps to be Self Accepting, and to adjust expectations. You can realize how you can hit a good forehand, but need to improve the ability to hit several in a row, and to do it when on the run. Being in the Learning Frame is important here. As you adjust your expectations it is easier to enjoy the process. With discouragement about match outcomes, it helps to be in a Curiosity Frame, being interested in discovering what is going on and how to get better. You can then come up with an improvement plan. Remember to enjoy the process of playing and learning.

RELATIONSHIP MANAGEMENT ISSUES: EXAMPLE 7

Issues: Nice guy, intimated by opponent, audience distraction issues, and game plan conflict with coach or teammate

Understanding the issues: Maybe you are a nice guy or gal who doesn't want your opponent to feel bad, so you lower your level. Or maybe you are afraid your opponent won't like you if you beat them. Alternatively, maybe you are intimidated by your opponent, either because of their behavior towards you or their stellar level of play. Another possibility is that you are distracted by friends, family or some other audience watching. This could lead you to change your game trying to impress them, or lose focus on your game plan. It could also happen that you have a coach or teammate or family person trying to give you a game plan you don't feel good about. Then you are torn about how to play, and that conflict hurts your play. All these issues require relationship management.

Using the NLP Outcome Frame experience organizing model:

Present State: lowering play level to not have opponent unhappy; tightening up due to feeling intimidated; attention on others watching me rather than playing my game; confused about how I should be playing

Desired State: play my game with my optimal mental state

Resources: You can be respectful of your opponent, treating them well, while still giving your best effort. Giving yourself permission to play well is important. Being a good person on the court doesn't mean you have to drop your level. In the example of an intimidating opponent, rather than get meek and tight, you might consider accessing your Determination to play the best you can. This is an attitude adjustment that can give you a chance to play your best. You are not trying to be an intimidator to them, but rather giving yourself a chance to play your best. In the case of spectators distracting, you need to play the game from your own eyes, not from their eyes seeing you. This means you are selecting and identifying how you want to play. If your coach wants you to play differently than you want, you may need to have a discussion with them about it, so you don't have jumbled energy and lowered commitment to your game playing. Each of the Relationship Management issues has you giving yourself permission to play your game, while also being the person you want to be.

EVENT MANAGEMENT SEQUENCE ISSUE: EXAMPLE 8

Issue: Insufficient Preparation

Understanding the issues: Our tennis is important to us, but somehow we often don't get our mind and body fully ready to play. Two issues here. One is to come up with a systematic routine. A systematic routine could address each of the Performance Categories: readying the Mental State, doing Physical State warm up, considering Game Plan, and Connecting to Strokes, for example. Secondly, do you take the time to do the warm up? We could know what to do to warm up, but it is too easy to not bother to do it, even though we know it is helpful. Here the issue is committing to take the time. Preparation can also have to do with what you are doing to ready for an event ahead of time. Do you have the sense of being "In Training", so you are working on readying your game?

Using the NLP Outcome Frame experience organizing model, an example is:

Present State: not ready to play physically

Desired State: physically warmed up and ready to play

Resources: Do your physical state readiness exercises before playing. If you've ever seen a boxing match, the boxer tends to enter the ring already sweating and ready to go. Do you have a systematic set of exercises you know to do to be ready to play physically? The same could be said for addressing the other Performance Categories.

EVENT MANAGEMENT SEQUENCE ISSUE: EXAMPLE 9

Issue: Not Adjusting During Matches

Understanding the issues: A big part of Self Coaching issues is to make Adjustments as needed. If your Self and Self Coach stay in communication, you can be in good position to make Adjustments in any needed Performance Categories. If you are losing and discouraged, and your Motivation dips, you can reconnect to your goals to pick up your Motivation. If your serve and volley game isn't working, do you make a switch to a baseline or junk game? If you are tense, do you calm yourself down? Are you monitoring your Performance Categories so you can make Adjustments as needed? If you are not making Adjustments during a match, it may be because you don't have your Self and Self Coach communicating as need be during the match. Do you know how to make Adjustments? Much of this training program has been to show you how to do this.

Using the NLP Outcome Frame, an example of making an Adjustment is:

Present State: hitting a tight backhand

Desired State: hitting the backhand the way I like

Resources: picturing my backhand the way I want to hit it with repetition. Have the Perspective: Focus on the Process, Don't Worry about the Outcome; notice and do this during the match

Using the NLP Outcome Frame experience organizing model for the problem of not making Adjustments during a match:

Present State: Not making Adjustments during a match; Self Coach not present and helping during a match

Desired State: Making Self Coach present and available to work with Self to monitor and make Adjustment during the match

Resources: Commit to having the Self Coach accessed and available during the match. Realize that a match includes being able to quickly step back to look at what is happening during the match. Remind self to monitor your Tennis Performance Categories, especially noticing if there is a problem or decline with any Performance Categories. There is time to do this between points and between games. If you have some issues that tend to pop up, pre match you can mentally rehearse making Adjustments on these issues. (Reminder if your Present State is going great and = your Desired State, no Adjustments are needed during that time.)

EVENT MANAGEMENT SEQUENCE ISSUE: EXAMPLE 10

Issue: Reviewing Match Too Self Critically

Understanding the issue: Too many players are too self critical after a match, commiserating with themselves derisively about their missed shots. Post match is a good time to review with joy the fun and interesting things that occurred during the match. Using the P-I-E (Praise, Improve, Encourage), you can remind yourself of what you did well (Praise), identify what you can do to get better (Improve), and come up with a plan for how to improve (Encourage).

Using the NLP Outcome Frame experience organizing model:

Present State: Not enjoying your good shots or opponents good shots in the match, or not seeing what you can work on to improve and coming up with a plan for it

Desired State: Enjoy having played and eager to work on things to improve

Resources: Use the P-I-E approach to enjoyably review your match.

The previous examples used the NLP Outcome Frame Organizing Model. Now we can use the Gestalt Therapy Concepts Organizing Model.

PHYSICAL STATE ISSUE: EXAMPLE 11

Issue: How to move better on the court

Understanding the issue: Getting older and not getting the desired push off on shots. Need to strengthen quads.

Using the Gestalt Therapy Concepts Organizing Model:

Awareness: Not getting the desired push off on returns, strokes, or moving to the ball. The quads don't seem strong enough.

Experiments: Experiment with a host of exercises to see what works. Try glute bridges; wall sits, move with bands across quads; check with physical therapist for more exercises; work on pushing off while playing. Each of the things mentioned is something to experiment with.

Contact: Check the quality of your push off, cycling back to more experiments if need be to get to your desired outcome

PERFORMANCE SKILLS ISSUE: EXAMPLE 12

Issue: Work on service motion

Understanding the Issue: After having had some physical injuries (hip replacement and rotator cuff surgery) I need to modify my motion for serving.

Awareness: Service motion isn't as consistent as before. Changing motion so all weight isn't on the front foot now.

Experiment: Can do a variety of experiments to discover what I want to do: experiment with ball toss; how much leaning into the court; how much racquet speed; how much spin vs how flat to hit it. Can experiment with each to check how it works for me

Contact: Check how fluid and reliable my serve is now

Here you actually cycle from Awareness (service motion off), to Experiment (ball toss a bit lower and tilting body, not so vertical), to Contact (make contact with the ball, feeling my balance and fluidity of the motion), to Awareness (like the forward feel, but the toss was a bit low), to Experiment (ball toss a bit higher but still with a body tilt into the court), to Contact (hit the serve solid but not much pop), Awareness (like the motion, but not enough pop), to Experiment (add racquet speed to the same serve, to Contact (hit the ball solid with good motion and speed).... So you see how this cycle works.

Sometimes the Self and Self Coach working together are uncertain how to proceed and decide to go inside to the inner self, the Unconscious, for help.

PERSONAL/PSYCHOLOGICAL ISSUE: EXAMPLE 13

Issue: Angry; Frustrated: Getting too upset about missing shots

Understanding the Issue: This player expects to make all her shots. She knows she knows how to play and expects to make all her shots. Telling her about the Learning Frame and doing Relaxation skills would work for a lot of players, but she still expects more of herself. She would like to not get so upset, but can't seem to get there. She feels stuck about how to fix this.

Inner Self Exploration experience processing model: She asks herself to go inside to discover what images, sensations, thoughts, or reactions emerge. She asks herself, "What do I need to know in order to not be so upset about missed shots?"

Inner Self message: She gets an image of years ago, as a child, learning a song on the piano. She made lots of mistakes at first, but that was ok. She didn't expect to have to know it right away. She recalls seeing her mom smiling and saying it was fun listening to her work on the song. After practicing a lot, she learned the song well.

Using the message: Transferring the learning from learning a song to developing in tennis. Trusting she will improve. Having the image of the learning process being ok and the warmth of her mom's smile enjoying her process, makes it possible to now give herself whatever time it takes to develop her game.

The messages you get from within often have a big impact.

The above are examples of how you can play Self Coach Tennis effectively. The examples could be endless. I hope you see your possibilities for managing your tennis experience favorably. You can see how we can apply various Models, Perspectives and Skills to help ourselves.

Chapter 10

Conclusion and Moving Forward

Be Your Own Best Self Coach
and Play Self Coach Tennis

BE YOUR OWN BEST SELF COACH

In this training we have worked on learning how to Self Coach effectively. To Self Coach well you need to understand the qualities of the Self Coach, with the Self Coach being welcoming, facilitative, wise, and cooperative, while having the inner resources to be supportive, activating, and directing/guiding. You need to understand the relationship between the Self and the Self Coach, and how you can communicate with yourself to have the experiences and outcomes you want. To be your best Self Coach it helps to have a base of Perspectives that can form a context for your being a participant in life events. I have provided you with a menu of wise Perspectives you can draw from to get you started on this. In terms of tennis, understanding the Tennis Performance Categories provides you with an understanding of the categories to monitor, adjust and improve on to play well. Understanding these Performance Categories helps you know what to attend to. In order to intervene well with yourself, in addition to Perspectives, it is important to know how to use Experience Organizing Models and Mental Skills that help you make sense of and maneuver well with your experience. Experience Organizing Models, like the NLP Outcome Frame, help you process and guide your experience clearly. Understanding possibilities for working with your unconscious wisdom, gleaned from reactions, dreams, images, sensations, feelings and thoughts, with cooperation between your Conscious and Unconscious Minds, further enables you to tap into your inner resources. We have done Mental Skills training to help you learn how to choose how to do things like talk with yourself, image things, and breathe and move choicefully. Your Mental State is vital to your functioning, providing a base of support, and lubricating/activating and guiding you to be able to function well, so we have done Mental State Training. You can now see the possibilities for selecting and managing your Mental States. We have also worked on the PAR Approach to the Event Management Sequence so you understand the tasks of Preparing, Adjusting and Reviewing for an event, and understand that your task is to do what you know, going for Par. Using these tools helps you not underperform, and provides you with the best possibilities for getting to a state of flow, and perhaps into the peak experience and peak performance zone.

Now it's your task to continue to develop the effective use of the models, perspectives and skills we have been training. As the joke goes: A person goes on a bus, and asks the bus driver, "how do you get to Carnegie Hall?". The bus driver answers, "Practice, practice, practice"

PLAY SELF COACH TENNIS

You now have the knowledge base and tools to become your own best Self Coach. To continue to develop, and to help your tennis performances, I invite you to play Self Coach Tennis. With Self Coach Tennis each time you play you commit to a process goal of using your Self Coaching models, perspectives, and skills, and then evaluating how you are doing. Just like you want to win your tennis match, you also want a good grade with your Self Coaching. For example, did you select a positive Perspective to key on for your match, and access a positive Mental State? Or, during the match, when your forehand tightened up, did you adjust by adopting the Focus on your Process, Don't Worry about the Outcome Perspective, and doing some muscle relaxation, while imaging yourself swinging freely? We can monitor things like how your Self and Self Coach are communicating, whether you are using an Experience Organizing Model, how you are doing selecting Self Coaching Perspectives, how you are accessing positive Mental States, and how you are working with the Tennis Performance Categories across an event, Preparing, Adjusting and Reviewing. The assumption is that having a positive self coaching process will mean your mental game is strong, which will help you be a better player, making the most of your abilities. You can rate/grade your Self Coaching, as well as your playing level when you play. It's not just about winning a match; it's also about developing your mental game through being an effective Self Coach.

To help you monitor, assess, and develop your Self Coaching there are a few checklists and rating scales you can fill out after you practice and play. You can fill out the Tennis Performance Category Checklist to see how you are doing with your Tennis Performance Categories. To understand your Mental States and Playing Level you can fill out the Mental State Playing Inventory, which includes the Playing Level Scale. To assess how you are doing with an overview of Self Coaching skills you can fill out the Self Coach Tennis (SCT) Rating Scale. Each of these can provide you with useful information for your understanding of how you are doing with your Self Coaching.

I hope you will find that playing Self Coach Tennis helps your experience and performance, helps you develop your game, and helps you be the person you want to be. Wishing you a great Self Coach Tennis journey!

Checklists and Rating Scales

**TENNIS PERFORMANCE CATEGORIES
CHECKLIST**

**MENTAL STATE PLAYING
INVENTORY**

**PLAYING LEVEL
SCALE**

**SELF COACH TENNIS (SCT)
RATING SCALE**

TENNIS PERFORMANCE CATEGORIES CHECKLIST
Neal Newman, Ph.D.

In order to perform well, it is important that you function well across a variety of performing categories. This includes categories such as your Mental State, Strokes, and Strategies, for example. Your task as a Self/Player and Self Coach is to monitor how well you are doing on these categories, coaching yourself to improve and perform as well as you can on each one. You can set goals for each performance, adjust during performances, and set goals for improving over time. On the following checklist you can rate from 1-10 how well you are managing each category, with 10 being best. You can rate this for your level in general on each ingredient, or you can rate the performance you just had. You can then set performance keys for the next play time, and performance goals for how you would like to improve.

Mental State Skills

Please rate the following on a 10 point scale, where 10 = major strength as a skill, and 1= lacking as a skill.

1. I know my best mental state. _____

2. I can step into my best mental state. _____

3. I can calm down when I need to. _____

4. I can energize/motivate myself. _____

5. I am a confident player. _____

6. I know how to boost my confidence. _____

7. I focus well. _____

8. I enjoy playing. _____

9. Nothing stops me from my best mental state. _____

10. I handle frustrations well. _____

11. What are your Mental State strengths and weaknesses?

12. Please describe your best playing Mental State, and how you access it.

13. Please identify what disrupts your best playing state, and how you deal with it.

Performance Skills – Tennis Strokes

Please rate your strokes on a 10 point scale, where 10 = very skilled, and 1 = low level of skills. You can use top players in your age group as your comparison group.

1. Forehand _____
2. Backhand _____
3. Serve _____
4. Forehand Return _____
5. Backhand Return _____
6. Forehand Volley _____
7. Backhand Volley _____
8. Overhead _____
9. Lob _____
10. Drop Shot _____

Please describe your Stroke strengths and weaknesses.

Strategy

Please rate your ability to handle strategy/game plan issues on a 10 point scale, where 10 = most skilled.

1. I know my own game. _____

2. I can design a game plan tailored to my opponent. _____

3. I can implement the game plan I select. _____

4. I can see patterns, and revise my game plan as needed. _____

5. I can play a forceful baseline game. _____

6. I can play a retrieving, counterpunching game. _____

7. I can play a serve and volley game. _____

8. I can play an all court game. _____

Please identify your Strategy strengths and weaknesses.

Physical State

Please rate how well developed you are on the following physical state issues on a 10 point scale, where 10 = most developed.

1. Strength _____
2. Speed, Agility, Quickness _____
3. Endurance/Conditioning _____
4. Flexibility _____
5. Timing/Feel _____
6. Health _____
7. Handling injuries/illness _____

Please describe your Physical State strengths and weaknesses.

Relationship Skills

Please rate your skills at managing relationships well while training or playing, on a 10 point scale, where 10 = most skilled.

1. Get along with coaches _____
2. Relate well with opponents/not intimidated _____
3. Cooperate well _____
4. Compete well _____
5. Handle audience/spectators well _____
6. Relate well with family about my tennis _____

Please describe your Relationship Skills strengths and weaknesses.

Environmental and External Factors

Please describe your ability to handle the following factors, where 10 = most skilled.

1. Environmental conditions (court surface, weather) _____
2. Equipment problems (break a string, string tension off, grip issues _____

Please describe your Environment and Equipment handling strengths and weaknesses.

Mental Skills

Please rate yourself on the following skills, where 10 = most skilled.

1. Ability to visualize how I want to play _____

2. Use mental rehearsal to prepare for matches _____

3. Use mental rehearsal to make adjustments during matches _____

4. Use positive self talk _____

5. Can draw on Self Coaching Perspectives _____

6. Can settle myself down as needed _____

7. Can guide myself effectively on the court _____

8. Can protect myself from adversity using protective devices _____

9. Set goals effectively.

Please describe your Mental Skills strengths and weaknesses.

Personal/Psychological Issues

Do you have any personal or psychological issues that you need to address and manage in order to play and enjoy a tennis event? Please describe.

MENTAL STATE PLAYING INVENTORY
Neal Newman, Ph.D.

Managing our Mental State (MS) is a vital part of Self Coaching Tennis. As such, we can give special attention to how we are doing with our MS. We can think of it as playing Mental State Tennis as well as Self Coach Tennis. As such, let's focus on doing a good job managing our MS, having that be an important process goal. The Self Coaching Tennis (SCT) Rating Scale, found elsewhere in this training, is a tool for monitoring how we are doing with our Self Coaching across the board of tasks. The Mental State Playing Inventory is a way to zoom in more on how we are doing with our MS while playing specifically.

MENTAL STATE PROFILE: We will here be rating Mental State relevant issues on a 10 point scale, where 10 = best, and 1 = worst. At times you will be asked to describe what was going on in terms of your mental state experience and playing.

1. Let's begin by assessing your MS while playing today with your Mental State Profile today. Please rate your Mental States while playing today/or for a certain event. Use a 10 point scale, where 10 = best, optimal level of a mental state, and 1 = low, worst level. After listing and rating the Core Mental States, there is room to add other mental states that you deem important, like Energetic, Playful, Fierce, or other words that you feel most importantly describe how you played. If you have very high levels of a MS, but think it got you in trouble, you can add a (+), like 10+, to indicate overconfidence, too relaxed, etc)

   Relaxed _____

   Concentration _____

   Confidence _____

   Motivation _____

   Determination _____

Enjoyment _____

Patience _____

Imperturbable (Unbothered by things) _____

Other _____ _____

Other _____ _____

Other _____ _____

2. Please describe what you notice about your MS Profile for this event. Are there MS that seemed especially high or low? Did it seem like a certain MS was important to getting the rest of the mental states to go up or down? Anything else you notice?

3. Rate your MS in general today _____

4. I accessed a positive MS to start the match _____

5. I maintained a positive MS throughout the match _____

6. I made adjustments to my MS as needed during the match

_____

7. Please describe anything important you notice about your ability to access, maintain and adjust your MS through this event.

PLAYING LEVEL SCALE

Our Mental State Profile gives us a sense of how our mental states are operating during a match, with an indicator of how optimal/positive our MS is. We can also look at our Playing level, where we give ourselves a rating of how On or Off our game we are for the event. I believe our task is to Self Coach so that we get to at least a PAR level. The concept of PAR, coming from golf, is that if we do the basic skills of the game effectively, we will score a par on the whole. So, if we know how to play well, and hit the shots we already know, we play at a par level. What if your level of tennis, though, does not include being able to hit all shots effectively and with repetition? In the PAR approach to tennis, when rating our level of play today, we realize our task is to do what we are currently capable of doing. We can set an improvement plan to raise our level of play for the future, but our task in today's event is to play at our PAR level at this time. Your PAR level isn't just the average of how you play, because you may be underperforming in events. Your PAR level is based on a reasonable assessment of how you know how to play now. If I can consistently hit 6 out of 10 backhand returns in the court in practice and practice sets, I am at my PAR if I do that in a match. We are checking on whether you are ON Your game now. Not underperforming. The premise is that if we do effective Self Coaching, we can increase our chances of playing up to PAR. Since effective Self Coaching puts us in an optimal mental state, we also create conditions for playing even better than PAR, in a flow state, and may even on occasion get into a zone of peak performance/experience.

In the Playing Level Scale, a 6 point scale, we are way OFF our game at 1, not terrible but still underperforming at 2, pretty ok at 3 but not quite doing what I can do, and ON at 4, which is our PAR. We are even more On at 5, which is in a flow state, and 6, which is transcendent zone of peak experience/performance. Getting to a 6 is special, but tends to be rare, so we could look at this as primarily a 5 point scale. The hope is that with effective Self Coaching you can very much reduce playing at a 1 or 2, and increase times you can play at a 4 or better more consistently. So, here is the Playing Level Scale:

PLAYING LEVEL SCALE: Please rate your playing level for this match or practice on basically a 5 point scale, but allow for a 6 for extraordinary occasions:

1 = OFF—way off my game, mental state disconnected—could be tense, unfocused, unconfident, unmotivated, discouraged, frustrated or angry

2 = UNDERPERFORMED—underperformed, but not the worst I could play; playing below average, but not terrible—maybe a little tight, less than fully confident, didn't miss every shot, but inconsistent, without best timing, maybe a bit frustrated or discouraged

3 = PLAYING JUST OK—playing ok, but know I can play better; play seems average, but not my best; can make some ok shots, but don't have full timing; may have some motivation, but not fully confident, comfortable and focused

4 = ON—ON PAR—on my game; mental state positive; feeling relaxed, confident, focused, motivated and enjoying, with good energy

5 = ON—Flow state—everything clicking automatically; racquet feels like part of me; in the moment fully, embracing the challenges with positive energy and mental state: relaxed, confident, enjoying, and focused

6 = IN THE ZONE—peak experience; peak performance—may have some extra positive transcendent experience—perhaps things seem to slow down, so can't miss; experience something extra special, something extraordinary

My Playing Level for this match/practice/event = _____

If your playing level varied a lot throughout a match you can give yourself more than one score. If, for example, you played awesome the first 2 sets, which you split with your opponent, and then your playing level dropped dramatically in the 3rd set, with physical state, mental state and strokes declining, you might give yourself a 4 for the first 2 sets, and a 2 for the 3rd set.

You might give yourself between a 3 and 4 for the whole match, but that wouldn't tell the whole story. In this example, you can rate this way:

My Playing Level for the first set = _____

My Playing Level for the second set = _____

My Playing Level for the 3rd set = _____

My Playing Level overall for the match = _____

We can take the information from our Mental State Profile and our Playing Level Scale to understand how our mental states are operating when we play well and less well. We can determine what to key on in a match as well as what elements of our mental states need work for improvement. Based on your latest playing, what do you want to key on next in your play?

SELF COACH TENNIS (SCT) RATING SCALE
Neal Newman, Ph.D.

The SCT Rating Scale is designed to help you monitor how effectively you are Self Coaching. This can serve as a reminder to use the models, perspectives, and skills taught in this SCT training program, and a help in guiding your practicing what you are learning. As you rate each item, you can discover what you are already using and adept at, and also see what you need to practice. The idea is to commit to SCT with your goal being to be able to masterfully work with yourself to achieve your outcomes for practicing and playing and being the person you want to be when involved in an event. Please rate each item on a 10 point scale, where 1 = no use, very low use or unhelpful use and 10 = very effective use, with the SC skill or perspective being used adroitly and masterfully.

SCT-General SC Processes—Models, Perspectives, Skills
Rating (1-10, 10 = best)

_____ I understand I am both a Self/Player and Self Coach when I play tennis

_____ My Self and Self Coach are working well together to help me manage playing

_____ My Self Coach (SC) is positive, being wise, welcoming, supportive, facilitative and guiding as needed

_____ I am using an Experience Organizing Model, where I identify my Present State, set my Desired State and facilitate accessing Resources that help me get to my Desired State

_____ My SC helps Support me, being understanding, kind, patient and self accepting

_____ My SC helps Activate me to have positive energy and a positive Mental State, with positive focus, intensity, motivation and determination

_____ My SC helps Direct/guide me to be able to set goals and access resources that will help me reach those goals

SCT—Self Coaching Perspectives

_____ My SC helps me have a positive frame of mind, by drawing on useful SC Perspectives

(Like the Learning, Opportunity, Challenging, Curiosity and Healthy frames, etc)

Please list the SC Perspectives you find most useful _____

_____

SCT—Mental Skills

_____ I am using positive self talk

_____ I am using imagery to positively affect me

_____ I am using movement, breathing, and muscle relaxation to help my mental state

_____ I use protective devices to keep me from being bothered by outside adversity or frustrations, such as plexiglass shield, force field, bubble, and step back

SCT—Mental States

_____ I understand my optimal Mental State

_____ I can access my optimal Mental State

_____ I can make Adjustments with my Mental State during a match

Please describe what you are understanding as important about your Mental State:_____

_____

_____

SCT—Tennis Performance Categories

_____ I understand where I am in terms of my Tennis Performance Categories—Mental State, Strokes, Strategy, Physical State, Relationship Management, Dealing with Environment and Equipment, Personal issues affecting playing

_____ I am managing my Performance Categories issues well during my playing times

_____ I have an improvement plan for handling my Performance Categories issues

Please describe your most important Tennis Performance Categories issues now:_____

_____

_____

SCT—The PAR Event Management Sequence

_____ I am Preparing well to play, getting myself mentally and physically ready, and readying my Tennis Performance Categories

_____ I am Adjusting my Tennis Performance Categories as needed while playing

_____ I am Reviewing my playing positively post playing using the P-I-E approach—Praise, Improve, Encourage. This allows me to enjoy the playing and set improvement goals.

SCT—Personal Issues: working through personal issues affecting performance

_____ I do not have personal issues affecting my ability to compete effectively

_____ I understand my personal issues affecting my competing and am handling them well

SCT—Goals Rating (1-10, 10 = best)

I am having a positive experience playing   _____

My SC helps me play better   _____

My SC helps me set improvement goals and plans   _____

My SC helps me be the person I want when I play   _____

Give yourself a Playing and Self Coaching grade for your practicing or playing today, where A = best, and F = worst.

Playing Grade today _____   Self Coaching Grade today _____

Describe your key points for improving your Self Coaching for the next time you play. What do you need in order to play better, and how can you coach yourself better?

Bibliography

Bandler, Richard & Grinder, John, *Frogs into Princes: Neuro Linguistic Programming*, (1979), Real People Press, Utah

Cheek, David, (1993), *Hypnosis: The Application of Ideomotor Techniques*, Allyn & Bacon

Csiksentmihaly, Mihalyi, *Flow: The Psychology of Optimal Experience*, (2008), Harper Perennial Modern Class Paperback

Dilts, Robert, DeLozier, Judith, with Deborah B Dilts, *NLP II: The Next Generation* (2010), Meta Publications, California

Gallwey, W. Timothy, *Inner Tennis*, (1976), Random House

Gallwey, W. Timothy, *The Inner Game of Tennis* (1987), Random House

Gilbert, Brad & Jamison, Steve, Winning Ugly (1994), Touchstone Publisher

Gilligan, Stephen, *Generative Trance* (2019), Crown House Publishing

Hill, Richard & Rossi, Ernest, *A Practitioner's Guide to to Mirroring Hands* (2018), Crown House Publishing

Horn, Thelma S.(Editor), *Advances in Sport Psychology*, (2008), Human Kinetics

Jackson, Susan & Csiksentmihalyi, Mihalyi, *Flow in Sports*, (1999), Human Kinetics

Loehr, James, & Tony Schwartz, (2005), *The Power of Full Engagement*, Free Press

Murphy, Michael, *In the Zone: Transcendent Experience in Sports* (1995), Penguin Group USA

Murphy, Michael, *The Future of the Body* (1993), Penguin Publishing Group

Newman, Mildred, & Berkowitz, Bernard, with Owen, Jean, *How to be your own best friend,* (1974), Ballantine Books

Nideffer, Robert, *An Athlete's Guide to Mental Training,* (1985), Human Kinetics

O'Connor, Joseph, *NLP & Sports,* (2001), Harper Collin's Publishers, London

O,Connor, Joseph & Seymour, John, *Introducing Neuro-Linguistic Programming,* (1990), Harper Collin's Publishers, London

O'Hanlon, William, (1987), *Taproots: Underlying Principles of Milton Erickson's Therapy and Hypnosis,* W.W. Norton

Peterson, Christopher, & Seligman, Martin, (2004), *Character Strengths and Weaknesses,* Oxford University Press, USA

Polster, Erv, & Polster, Miriam, (1973), *Gestalt Therapy Integrated,* Bruner/Mazel

Reik, Theodore, (1948), *Listening with the Third Ear,* Grove Press

Rossi, Ernest, *The Symptom Path to Enlightenment* (1996), Palisades Gateway Publishing

Rossi, Ernest, *The Psychobiology of Gene Expression* (2002), W.W.Norton Professional Books, New York

Zinker, Joseph, *Creative Process in Gestalt Therapy,* (1977), Bruner/ Mazel Publishers, New York

About the Author

Neal Newman, Ph.D., was raised in New York City, where he attended the H.S. of Music & Art. After attending Earlham College in Richmond, Indiana, he got his doctorate in Counseling Psychology from Ohio State University, where he also completed an APA accredited internship in Clinical Psychology at the Ohio State University Medical Center. Neal is retired  from the Ohio State University Counseling & Consultation Service. He also has a small private practice in Columbus, Ohio. Neal has had significant training and experience in Neuro-Linguistic Programming (NLP), Ericksonian approaches, and Gestalt Therapy. Over the years Neal has done a lot of sport psychology and performance enhancement work with tennis players, other athletes, musicians, and the general population. Neal has also been an accomplished tennis player, who has won 40 USTA national doubles titles, 4 ITF world championship doubles titles, and represented the U.S. internationally numerous times, including being a member of two teams that won the ITF world team championship. Neal has been ranked #1 nationally in doubles across multiple senior age groups and in father-son tennis with his son, Cole. Neal has been inducted into the USTA Midwest Hall of Fame. Neal is married to Rayna. They have a daughter Jen, a son Cole, who is married to Becky, and a grandson Caiden. Neal's mom and step-dad were Mildred Newman and Bernard Berkowitz, who were psychoanalysts and co-authors of the best seller *How To Be Your Own Best Friend*.

www.ingramcontent.com/pod-product-compliance
Lightning Source LLC
Chambersburg PA
CBHW071733120626
46550CB00002B/505

* 9 7 9 8 9 9 9 2 6 9 7 3 0 8 *